The Antichrist Son of Satan

Half Devil Half Man

ERIKA GREY

Pedante Press

Short Book Series

004

All Scriptural quotations in this publication are from the New King James Version of the Bible © by Thomas Nelson, Inc.

Printed in the United States of America

Copyright © 2020 Erika Grey

All rights reserved.

ISBN: ISBN: 978-1-940844-16-9

DEDICATION

To you, my readers.

CONTENTS

	Acknowledgments	i
1	The Cold Chill of a Demon	1
2	Satan's Hierarchy	11
3	The Antichrist Entity	41
4	The Bottomless Pit & The Restrainer	63
5	Tribe of Dan and Satan	76
6	Lion of Bashan - Nephilim	91
7	Birth-Bloodline of Antichrist	105
8	Rising From Europe	116
9	The Science of God-Angels-Demons-666	128
10	What This Means For the Tribulation Saints	163

www.erikagrey.com

For Bible Prophecy news and analysis and more books visit my website.

1 THE COLD CHILL OF A DEMON

A Passage in Leviticus

Years ago, in the beginning of my research, I held the view that the Antichrist referred to a man born of a woman in the usual way. Many theologians and Bible scholars taught this idea, though not all. After writing many articles and books, which included a good deal of Biblical research, my view took a radical turn. It was a passage in a most seemingly unrelated portion of Scripture that provided my switch in direction: the book of Leviticus. More on this passage later.

This report supports the finding that the Antichrist is the actual son of Satan. This means a supernatural birth with Satan himself as his father. Just as Jesus the son of God walked the earth, so also will the Antichrist, Satan's son. Both born of women, one a virgin birth. Jesus was God and man. The Antichrist is a devil and man. He is also not just any devil as you will discover. Jesus originates from heaven, the other from a place one would not expect, that will leave you completely horrified.

This work reveals Satan's hierarchy and provides a detailed view into the demonic realm, more so than in any other work on the topic. In addition, the report solves several Biblical mysteries including the "restrainer" mentioned in 2 Thessalonians 2:6. Finally this book provides a view into the science of demons. It concludes with the discovery of the full meaning of the image of the beast and what 666 represents. Yes, the mystery of the ages is revealed in this expose. You will understand why the Tribulation saints will rather die than take the Antichrist's mark. Moreover, why taking it means eternal death.

The Cold Chill of a Demon

While writing this work, I experienced many Satanic attacks, which caused delays for this work's completion. One sunny, spring day a chill came around me that was so frigid, I could not get warm, I had never experienced such cold, I was doing everything I could to heat up. I realized it was an unusual chill: freezing. In the mix of that day's hinderances, this was a demon that came to me directly.

I had felt the chill of the presence of a spirit before. Once while praying one out of a young male who was encountering evil obtrusive thoughts. Another was in a video game that my son left in my downstairs' closet. The room had a cold, eerie feel. In one area I felt the unmistakable chill. I went looking and found several items, but one that caught my attention was a video game named Diablo, which is Spanish for Devil. I destroyed the game and prayed the demon out and felt the icy being as it left. Once gone, warmth entered the room and the eerie feel and cold was gone.

Afterwards when walking by the entertainment section of a store, I could feel the demonic presence in the section of Diablo games.

My Experience with Demons

Prior to my becoming a born-again Christian,

as a young adolescent I took a science elective course on the paranormal. In the class audio tapes of demons were played. I can still hear the guttural growls and horrific scratching. In addition, the teacher showed our group pictures of ghosts.

Unbeknownst to me I was training to become a medium. A woman came to class one day and taught how to talk to the spirits. She emphasized placing a bowl of water in the room because the spirits are attracted to it. Having been given this information, I held a seance with my friends. We all joined hands in a circle. With all our eyes closed I could tell when the circle was broken meaning someone was not concentrating. I tape recorded the event.

We all heard what sounded like a small girl let out a scream as if she were falling off a cliff. The tape recorded it. I later learned this was demons performing miracles. Revelation 16:14 talks about demons working miracles for Satan via the three spirit like frogs. This applies to all other devils as well. They also work wonders for Lucifer. Some appear as ghosts, others as aliens, all to lead people astray from the truth.

Later when I became a born-again Christian right before my 18th birthday paranormal occurrences took place as if the demons that had influenced my life were angry at my conversation. Soon after their antics stopped.

My experience with the demonic oppressed

My experience with the supernatural has allowed me to know things no one could possibly know. For instance, when someone was dangerous. A young man with serious mental health issues and drug addiction showed me a homemade tattoo he designed of an evil clown with horns. As he was smiling shockingly the face of the evil clown came through his own and he had unknowingly designed the demon that kept him in his prison house.

In another case a woman wanted me to see a tattoo on her boyfriend, the design deeply disturbed her. She brought him to me. I told the man there was an extremely evil spirit that he had given himself to and it had a strong hold over him. She soon discovered that he was out of prison for molesting and sexually abusing the children of a woman he married.

On one occasion I knew an act a young girl would commit based on the demon I sensed was inside of her. I knew she was dangerously unpredictable and capable of impulsive violence. Days from meeting her I learned she threw rocks though the windows at her school and was carted off by ambulance workers. I also learned that she had been in a mental hospital strapped to a bed prior to joining the classmates at the school she briefly attended.

I saw a demon over a family member who would soon after struggle with a form of anorexia. She became addicted to Adderall for the soul purpose of controlling her weight. Oddly for a time she painted variations of the first demon I saw over her. Later I saw another demon with skull like features with a largely distorted smile, this was distortion, to make her see her see her body as distorted. It did not surprise me when she told me that her issue was not exactly anorexia but body dysmorphia.

Eyes and Images of Demons

I have seen the evil demonic eyes that come through people's eyes. In addition to witnessing their faces take on those of the spirits who afflict them. I have felt entities in objects, and strongholds that take over buildings. I also can feel those that reside over towns and cities. A couple stood out to me for their absolute strength: the city of Rome and the European Union Parliament building.

Face of Death

Moreover, I saw the face of the principality Death, that God allowed me to see as I was studying Revelation 6. Theologians stated that Death was a figurative illustration, but I was reading something different. After praying about this mystery, a face appeared as I closed my eyes. I sat up in horror. Without a doubt I knew it was the face of Death. God allowed me to see him to understand that he is a major principality.

Death is a demonic entity near the top of Satan's hierarchy. Death's features were of a skeleton face of a creature not of this world, it was the most frightening of faces. He wore a black shroud. I understood after seeing Death, that his image is everywhere in Halloween and in heavy metal rock: that is skeletons with shrouds and black robes.

Heavenly Visions

On the other side of the evil I have seen heavenly visions. I saw a Godly hedge of fire around my daughter as she was about to enter a dangerous period of her life. When I worried, I remembered the vision as a promise of God's safety for her.

Most unusual was when my mother was dying, and we were around her bed during the death vigil. No one can know when someone is about to die. Even as the breathing changes the death process still takes time. My mother was in a coma. Her eyes were closed. She had sepsis and the front of her nose was open and raw. It started as irritation from the oxygen tube in her nostrils. It turned to infection and spread. The nurse while turning her dropped her on her face and this opened the wound even more.

Disease and death are a horrible, ugly process. From having small cell lung cancer, she now had a raw open nose as if the disease were now eating her flesh. While I sat next to her, during the vigil, suddenly, I felt this incredible presence enter the room. I had never felt anything like it before; a wonderful feeling of joy, happiness, peace all rolled into one. I knew her moment had come, and it was either Jesus or angels that had now come for her. I said, "Mom, Jesus is here for you now. It's time for you to go." Shockingly her eyes opened, and she was gazing and looking up. My sister grabbed her shoulder and screamed, "She is not going anywhere."

I watched her face as her soul was departing, she had this glow and her nose looked normal as she gazed into the upper corner of the room. As she beheld the glory of God through what entered the room her face appeared flawless, her nose appeared healed. Two or three times she uttered very quietly with a body near death as if with the last breath she could muster, "God, God, God."

Meanwhile I was praying as both Jesus and Stephen, although I did not have to, "Lord into your hands I command her spirit." Just when it seemed her end had finally come, there was one last movement with her mouth and then her body relaxed into death. Immediately those in the room started to weep bitterly while all I felt was ecstatic joy. She had only departed this earth and a glorious departure at that.

Understanding the spiritual realm

God would use all these experiences to help me to understand and write about the demonic and heavenly world that these pages detail. While there are many more I could have added, this book's focus is the Satanic hierarchy at the highest levels. Including the entity that is the Antichrist: the son of Satan. From the observations I relayed I would question why I was able to feel demons but not see them. Why are they cold? How come you can see the eyes or glimpses of the features as it inhabits a person? All these questions will be answered, and it ties into the spirit of the Antichrist, and the frightening truth this book will reveal.

Of all my works this one goes to the depths of darkness and into the scientific realm of the supernatural. Even I had to stop writing this work several times. This is the material for nightmares. We cannot fully imagine what it is going to mean for those living on the earth at the time of the Antichrist's reign. Not to mention the frightful end of this book, that I sat in horror upon my discovery.

2 SATAN'S HIEGHARCHY

Satan was the highest of angels: a covering cherub. He walked on the mountain of God, through fiery stones, a heavenly beautiful fire, not like an earthy flame. The word in the Bible used for this fire means a supernatural fire.

Fire in the Bible represents the Holy Spirit, it is a symbol of purity and of God's power and holiness. God speaks of being a wall of fire for Israel in Zechariah 2:5. It exists in the supernatural realm with a different significance than physical fire. When Ezekiel saw the four living creatures who are before God's throne, they appeared amidst a cloud of a raging heavenly fire (Ezekiel 1:4).

In Revelation 15:2 the Tribulation martyrs are seen standing on the sea of glass mingled with fire. When Elijah saw the invisible army, they appeared as chariots of fire.

Ezekiel 28:14 states that Lucifer was the cherub who covers. The word cakak in the Hebrew means, to hedge, defend, block, overshadow, cover, to protect. Jonathan Edwards wrote that Lucifer was designed to cover or protect man in the garden. He and others suggested that Lucifer did not like being man's guardian and in addition he rivaled Christ.

Lucifer-Perfection of Beauty

While we do not understand exactly what Satan protected. It could mean that he was over all of the angels. We know that he ranked within the heavenly top tier of seraphim, and the four living creatures. He was the cherub of the Garden of Eden, God's garden (Ezekiel 28:13.)

Lucifer was nicknamed by God, "Son of the Morning" or "Morning Star." Meaning he shined the brightest among angels. This title of Lucifer's compares to Jesus. His is the bright and morning star that outshines all others. But this explains why theologians theorize Satan rivaled Christ. The similarity also reveals Lucifer's high position. Among the angels he ranked first among them as the dawn again like Jesus's name. Whereas Jesus' star indicates Venus. In addition, Jesus is known by many other titles.

God gave Lucifer more wisdom and knowledge than the other angels. In addition, God made him extremely beautiful. One could only imagine what it was like to look at him. One who is "perfect in beauty." Ezekiel 28: 12 states, "You were the seal of perfection, Full of wisdom and perfect in beauty." He was the angel over the archangels. He was given considerable knowledge of God's universe.

Satan had a throne in heaven with God as a high-ranking angel as top tier officials sit in government.

In Isaiah 14:13 Lucifer refers to his throne and states, "I will exalt my throne above the stars of God." In Revelation 20:4 John confirms the thrones by stating, "And I saw thrones, and they sat upon them, and judgement was given unto them." Psalm 122:5 confirms, "For there are set thrones of judgement, the thrones of the house of David." Daniel 7:9 adds, "I beheld till the thrones were cast down, and the Ancient of days did sit." We see Satan's throne later referenced by Jesus in Revelation 2:12. It is now on earth. Scholars agree it sits in Pergamum.

The Angelic Fall

According to Isaiah 14: 12-14, Lucifer wanted to be like God and determined to surpass Him. He was then cast out of the mountain of God. According to Revelation 12:4 Lucifer took a third of the angels with him to the earth. He was renamed Satan, which means adversary.

While the Bible does not tell us we can assume as with the fall of man so also with angels. Transformations took place in man's nature and in his body. Most likely once Lucifer sinned changes ensued in him and in the Angelic host who fell from grace. We see this evidenced in the description of Lucifer in his angelic glory, described as shining as jewels, to a fiery red dragon. At his end, he looks ordinary which shocks the nations who see him.

Isaiah 14:16 states, "Those who see you will gaze at you, And consider you, saying, "Is this the man who made the earth tremble, Who shook kingdoms?" Based on Scriptures angels appear as men as well as having other forms intrinsic as part of their beings. The Bible refers to them as stars. Jesus stated that he saw Satan fall from heaven like a flash of lightening.

The Scripture tells us that Satan was cast out of the mountain of God as profane and cut down. At this event, the fallen heavenly host changed from beautiful heavenly creatures to ugly, ghastly looking, ice cold and foul beings. They became visually grotesque as the sin they represented. Never-the-less, they could also appear as an angel of light.

The War Between God and Satan

Thus, the war between Satan and God was launched. Among the third of angels Satan took with him, were archangels along with those who became demons or messengers and ministers for Satan.

In addition to Satan and his demons grieving God by doing all that He hates, their ultimate plan was to capture God's next creation: man. Man was created a little lower than the angels and was to dwell with God in the Garden. The trees in the Garden were DNA changing trees. Satan knew this. If he could get Eve to eat the fruit, he would achieve a major win. When Eve ate from the tree of the knowledge of good and evil, it changed man's original DNA to bring in spiritual and physical death. Once the fall occurred, former archangels Death and Hades would have a major role.

From here demons would issue lies to keep man from the knowledge of the true God. In addition, they would seek to get man to sin and steal from his life and destroy it.

According to definition of the Biblical word used for demons, it defines as an inferior pagan deity. "Demons" are spiritual agents acting in all idolatry. The idol itself is nothing, but every idol has a "demon" associated with it who induces idolatry, with its worship and sacrifices. Their mission, to turn man from the true God.

In addition, demons would seek to enslave men and women in spiritual prisons of darkness. For example, through mental illness addiction and various sins. Those who did not end in Satan's prison, they would work hard to deceive. Ultimately, they wanted man's death without Christ. Their goal was to obtain as many souls as possible. Death would take their lives and Hades would provide a home to the forever lost souls.

Jesus and the New Birth

After the fall, God provided a way back to fellowship with Him and eternal life. It would come through the birth, death, and resurrection of the Lord Jesus Christ. By the shedding of His blood would come the remission of sins. A new birth in Christ, a spiritual one. One would receive the Holy Spirit to teach, guide and confirm their life in Christ. The coming of Jesus was foretold in the Garden. He would crush the head of Satan. Satan's counter in part included the spirit of Antichrist.

Symbolism of Eating-Lord's Supper

We see a comparison to the Lord's supper relating to the fall. It was through the act of eating man fell and wrought in eternal damnation. In the Lord's supper the partaking of the body and blood of Jesus via the bread and the wine represents the symbolic eating that negates the death ushered in from the fall.

John 6:54-56 states, "Whoever eats my flesh and drinks My blood has eternal life, and I will raise him up at the last day. For My flesh is food indeed, and My blood is drink indeed. He who eats My flesh and drinks My blood abides in Me, and I in him."

We see the symbolic meal first commanded by God in Exodus 12 for the Passover meal. The lamb represented the coming Messiah, or Jesus, along with the unleavened bread and bitter herbs. The blood on the door of Passover depicted the coming Messiah's blood that would be shed for the remission of their sins. Another symbolic act like the Lord's supper, but with spiritual significance.

Eating forbidden fruit ushered in death. The symbolic partaking of the blood and body of Christ represents the reconciliation from the fall and new life found in the shed blood of the Messiah or Jesus Christ. Not to mention the same representation in the consuming of the Jewish offerings. We see Satan's counter of these in the idol sacrifices and meals. In Revelation 2:14 Jesus admonishes , "But I have a few things against, you, because you have those who hold the doctrine of Balaam, who taught Balak to put a stumbling block before the children of Israel, to eat things sacrificed to idols, and to commit sexual immorality."

In line with the idea of eating as a symbol of spiritual death in the garden, and of life in Christ is the teaching of Christ as the last Adam. 1 Corinthians 15:45-49 confirms:

"And so it is written, "The first man Adam became a living being." The last Adam became a life-giving spirit. However, the spiritual is not first, but the natural, and afterward the spiritual. The first man was of the earth, made of dust; the second Man is the Lord from heaven. As was the man of dust, so also are those who are made of dust; and as is the heavenly Man, so also are those who are heavenly. And as we have borne the image of the man of dust, we shall also bear the image of the heavenly Man."

The Antichrist as a mocker of the Lord Jesus Christ will pervert even this aspect of His divine person as a counter to Him. Through the mark of the beast he will seek to merge man with machines and especially his infrastructure. He might even tout it as the path to eternal life.

Principalities, Powers and Armies

God refers to Himself many times in the Bible as the Lord of Hosts, and this means armies. These rank in positions of power just like commanders and soldiers. We see this with the appearance of the Commander of the Lord's Army in Joshua 5:13 -15, which reads:

And it came to pass, when Joshua was by Jericho, that he lifted his eyes and looked, and behold, a Man stood opposite him with His sword drawn in His hand. And Joshua went to Him and said to Him, "Are You for us or for our adversaries?" So He said, "No, but as Commander of the army of the Lord I have now come." And Joshua fell on his face to the earth and worshiped, and said to Him, "What does my Lord say to His servant?" Then the Commander of the Lord's army said to Joshua, "Take your sandal off your foot, for the place where you stand is holy." And Joshua did so.

The Scriptures only provide glimpses into this army. We see it in Jude 9, with the reference of the dispute over Moses' body between Michael the archangel and Satan.

We also see it with war that will take place in heaven. Daniel 12:1 foretells, "At that time Michael, shall stand up, The great prince who stands watch over the sons of your people; And there shall be a time of trouble, Such as never was since there was a nation, Even to that time." This corresponds with Revelation 12:7, "And war broke out in heaven' Michael and his angels fought with the dragon; and the dragon and his angels fought, but they did not prevail, nor was a place found for them in heaven any longer."

The Higher the Rank, the Greater the Power

In the angelic realm the higher the rank the greater the powers The Scripture also references demons more powerful. In addition to those with greater evil. We also see that principalities of preeminence have angels beneath them. Revelation 12:7 highlighted 'Michael and his angels" fighting the dragon and his angels. The third of the angels that Satan took, provide the numbers for his army. This is a considerable number. Satan was over the archangels and we know of at least several that joined him. Some of them ended up in the Abyss under lock and key.

Satanic Power Structure

We get a glimpse of the naming of the power structure of angels and demons. Ephesians 1:21 states that Jesus's power is "Far above all principality, and power, and might, and dominion, and every name that is named, not only in this world, but also in that which is to come." In the Bible principality means, magistracy, chief, rule, power.

The Satanic Order

The highest positions in the Satanic order are the unholy trinity. While all three can be former cherubs, the Antichrist is most likely a former arch angel.

- **Satan**-Former Cherub-Highest angel, greater powers than an archangel.
- **Antichrist**-Former Archangel
- **False Prophet**-Former archangel or high-ranking demon
- **Death**-Former Archangel
- **Hades**-Former Archangel
- **Demons**-Former Angels
- **Spirits**-These include Holy and Evil and Spirits of God, Spirits of Satan.

Spirits in the Bible

Based on the Scriptures the word for spirit is also used interchangeably with demons. There are also degrees of their power. The definition of the word used for spirit in the Hebrew reflects its varied meaning. From pertaining to man's emotions, to his vitality, to God's Spirit, those issued by Him and evil beings.

While the word provides a lengthy description, I will only highlight some of the definitions such as wind, breath, mind spirit. Breath of air, air, gas, energy of life, and air in motion.

There are different spirits mentioned in the Bible. The first named is the Spirit of God, and the Spirit of the Lord. Along with Holy Spirit and its associated fruits, which characterize God and Jesus Christ. These are love, joy, peace, and patience.

The Demonic spirits on the other hand produce the opposite. For example, hate, greed, gluttony, addiction, discontent, jealousy, rage, anger, all kinds of sexual immorality and more. Lying spirits are also numerous. God Himself even sends these in response to unbelief. 2 Thessalonians references the demonic power during the Tribulation along with the delusion that God will send. It states, "The coming of the lawless one is according to the working of Satan, with all power, signs and lying wonders, and with all unrighteous deception among those who perish, because they did not receive the love of the truth, that they might be saved. And for this reason God will send them a strong delusion, that they should believe a lie, that they all might be condemned who did not believe the truth but had pleasure in unrighteousness."

God's Spirits

The spirits of God are difficult to understand. But, they relate to God's holiness. The seven spirits of God are mentioned in Revelation 1:4, 3:1 and 4:5 and 5:6. In addition to others possibly associated with God. Theologians have named the seven as those recorded in Isaiah 11:2:

- "The Spirit of the Lord shall rest upon Him,
- The Spirit of wisdom and understanding,
- The Spirit of counsel and might,

- The Spirit of knowledge and of the fear of the Lord."

Deuteronomy 34:9 records that Joshua had the spirit of wisdom.

In addition are the spirits of the four living creatures mentioned in Ezekiel 10:17, which describes of the wheels that rest alongside of them, "When the cherubim stood still, they also stood still, and when the cherubim rose, they rose with them, because the spirit of the living creatures was in them." The four living creatures relate to God's holiness and are little understood.

Satan has his spirits that counter God's. His are represented in the 3 spirits like frogs that come out of the mouths of each member of the unholy trinity.

Spirits of Jesus

There are also spirits in relation to Jesus. Isaiah 61:1 speaking of Jesus states, "The Spirit of the Lord God is upon me." We have here the mention of the Spirit of God upon Jesus. The following spirits are referred belonging to Jesus.

- Spirit of truth (John 14:17 John 16:14) referring to Jesus
- Spirit of Jesus Christ (Philippians 1:19)
- Spirit of Christ (1 Peter 1:11)
- Spirit of His Son (Galatians 4:6)
- Spirit of Prophecy (Revelation 19:10)
- Spirit of his Mouth (2 Thessalonians 2:8)
- Spirit of grace and supplications (Zechariah 12:10)
- Spirit of life (Romans 8:2) (in Christ)

The Satanic spirits that counter Jesus is the spirit of Antichrist in addition to the Antichrist himself. The spirit of Antichrist exists during the age of Grace, while he reigns in person during the final seven years of Israel.

Spirits Associated with the Holy Spirit

We see the Holy Spirit represented as fire. From the fiery cinnamon and cassia of the holy anointing oil God directed Moses to make, to the tongues of fire that came over the disciples at Pentecost (Acts 2:3).

Holy in the New Testament means sacred, pure, morally blameless, consecrated, sinless, and clean. Below is a list of Spirit most likely associated with the Holy Spirit. The Spirit of life might also be associated with Jesus.:

- Spirit of Truth (1 John 4:6)
- Spirit of life-Law of the (Romans 8:2) (in Christ)
- Spirit of meekness (1 Corinthians 4:21, Gal 6:1)
- Holy Spirit of Promise (Ephesians 1:13)
- Spirit of holiness (Romans 1:4)
- Spirit of Wisdom and Revelation (Ephesians 1:13)
- Faithful spirit (Proverbs 11:13)
- Eternal spirit (Hebrews 9:14)
- Spirit of adoption (Romans 8:5)
- Spirit of life (Revelation 11:11)

Holy Spirit

Of all three members of the Trinity, the Holy Spirit carries on many tasks and is probably the least understood.

Jesus was conceived by the power of the Holy Spirit, and of God coming upon Mary. Luke 1:35 describes, "And the angel answered and said to her, "The Holy Spirit will come upon you, and the power of the Highest will overshadow you; therefore, also, that Holy One who is to be born will be called the Son of God."

The Holy Spirit is a comforter and advocate. Jesus said in John 14;16, "And I will pray the Father, and He shall give you another Comforter, that He may abide with you forever."

The word used in the Greek is paracletos, which in English is paraclete and means comforter, advocate. In the wider sense it means a helper, aider, assistant, a succorer. This is a saver-as from danger or violence, a rescuer, a giver of help in time of need, that leads to a deeper knowledge of gospel truth. The Spirit also gives divine strength to undergo trials and persecutions on behalf of the kingdom of God.

The Holy Spirit sanctifies. Romans 15:16 affirms, "That I should be the minister of Jesus Christ to the Gentiles ministering the gospel of God, that the offering up of the Gentiles might be acceptable, being sanctified by the Holy Ghost."

The Holy Spirit teaches. Teaches 1 Cor 2:13

states, "These things we also speak, not in worlds which man's wisdom teaches but which the Holy Spirit teaches, comparing spiritual things with spiritual." John 14:26 adds, "But the Helper, the Holy Spirit, whom the Father will send in My name, He will teach you all things, and bring to your remembrance all things that I said to you." The Holy Spirit will bring the Word of God to our memory.

The Holy Spirit makes intercession for the believer. Romans 8:26 states, "Likewise the Spirit also helps us in our weaknesses. For we do not know what we should pray as we ought, but the Spirit Himself makes intercession for us with groanings which cannot be uttered."

The Holy Spirit Seals the Believer. Each believer receives gift of the Holy Spirit (Acts 2:38, Romans 5:5, Hebrew 2:4). Each is also sealed by the Holy Spirit. Ephesians 1:13 affirms, "In Him you also trusted, and after you heard the word of truth, the gospel of your salvation; in whom also, having believed, you were sealed with the Holy Spirit of promise.

The Holy Spirit can be grieved. Ephesians 4:30 affirms, "And grieve not the Holy Spirit of God, whereby you are sealed unto the day of redemption." This aspect of the Holy Spirit is intriguing. The word for grieved means, to make sorrowful, to affect with sadness, cause grief, throw into sorrow, to grieve, offend, to make one uneasy, and cause him a scruple. This defines as a feeling a doubt or hesitation regarding the morality or propriety of a course or action. In addition to being grieved, the Holy Spirit can be blasphemed.

Satan's demons work hard in spiritual warfare to counter the work of the Holy Spirit. They even trick Christians into thinking they are hearing from the Holy Spirit when they are hearing from Demons. During the Tribulation, the Antichrist will blaspheme the Holy Spirit.

Evil Spirits Mentioned in the Bible

Just as there are the spirits of the Holy Trinity in the Bible, Satan has his spirits or demons as well. As I stated some of these are locked in the Abyss. Below are all the evil spirits mentioned in Scripture. These first two we have already discussed:

Spirit of Antichrist (1 John 4:3)
Unclean spirits like Frogs (Revelation 16:3)

Demons are in the idols

The Bible makes it noticeably clear that demons are in the idols. This is an especially important Biblical teaching. It's also key in understanding the full impact of the mark of the beast discussed in detail in a later chapter

In Leviticus 17:7 God instructs the Israelites, "They shall no more offer their sacrifices to demons, after whom they have played the harlot..." Deuteronomy 32:17 reiterates, "They sacrificed to demons, not to God."
Paul elaborates on idolatry and demons in 1 Corinthians 10:19-21:" What am I saying then? That an idol is anything, or what is offered to idols is anything? Rather, that the things which the Gentiles sacrifice they sacrifice to demons and not to God, and I do not want you to have fellowship with demons. You cannot drink the cup of the Lord and the cup of demons; you cannot partake of the Lord 's Table and the table of demons."

This is also noticeably clear for the last days, end times and during the Tribulation. Revelation 9:21 reads, "But the rest of mankind, who were not killed by these plagues, did not repent of the works of their hands, that they should not worship demons, and idols of gold, silver, brass, stone, and wood, which can neither see nor hear nor walk. And they did not repent of their murders or their sorceries or their sexual immorality or their thefts." This gets self-evident when we look to the spirits of divination.

Spirit of divination (Acts 16:16)

In Hebrew the word used for divination is qacam, which means divine, diviner soothsayer, to practice divination, of diviners of nations, Balaam, of false prophets of Israel, prohibited, and determine by lot or magical scroll. The word is a verb always used of false prophets. But once we get to the Greek definition, we are provided further insight. In Acts 16:16 it states, "And it came to pass, as we went to prayer, a certain damsel possessed with a spirit of divination met us, which brought her masters much gain by soothsaying."

The word in the Greek used is Python. It derives from Puthon, the name of the region where the Oracle of Delphi was located. Python in Greek mythology was the Pythian serpent or dragon that dwelt in the region of

Pytho at the foot of Parnassus in Phocis and guarded the Oracle of Delphi. This was the most important shrine in all of Greece. It dates to 1400 BC.

Apollo, son of Zeus, and twin brother of the goddess Artemus, who was considered the god of the sun, healing, medicine. archery, music, poetry, justice and of prophecy killed Python.

As the story goes, there was a shrine to Themis, the goddess of telling the future. It was taken over by Python, the dragon who had tried to eat his mother. Apollo killed python and claimed Delphi as his temple. He got two sailors to be priests and gave a girl the power of telling the future. The girl became the priestess or oracle. The ancients viewed the the oracle as a messenger for the gods. The Oracle of Delphi was the most famous. The priestess of Apollo was called a Pythia. People came from all over Greece and beyond to have her answer their questions about the future. She spoke in riddles. Arguments over the interpretation were common. Scholars also congregated at the Delphi.

The spirit of the Oracle was a demon. As the Scripture states, the demons are in the gods.

Most likely how a mythological god is depicted, is what its demonic counterpart might look like.

A Familiar Spirit

A familiar spirit is a necromancer; one that evokes the dead. In modern language a medium. God speaks against these individuals who seeks these spirits to cut them off from His people. (Leviticus 19:31, 20:6, 20:27, Deuteronomy 18:11, 1 Samuel 28:3, 28:7, 1 1 28:8-9, 2 Kings 21:6, 23:24, 1 Chronicles10:13, 2 Chronicles 33:6, Isaiah 8:19, 19:3, 29:4)

In the Hebrew, the word for familiar spirt translates to water skin bottle, necromancer, one who evokes the dead, ghost, spirit of dead practice of necromancy, one that has a familiar spirit. It derives from the Hebrew word Owb from the idea of prattling a father's name, , a mumble, that is a water-skin (from its hollow sound) hence a necromancer (ventriloquist, as from a jar)—bottle, and a familiar spirt.

It continues the definition with a bottle, so called from carrying water, used of wine bottles. Like new bottles full of new wine which burst.

In addition it adds "a soothsayer, who evokes the manes of the dead by the power of incantations and magical songs, in order to give answers as to future or doubtful things; Specifically it denotes a soothsaying demon of which these men were believed to be possessed; a man or a woman when a python is in them. Divine to me by the familiar spirit, whence such a sorceress is called a woman in whom is a soothsaying demon.

It adds, "The dead person himself raised up; Isaiah 29:4 and they voice shall be as of a dead man rising from the earth. Almost always render by ventriloquists, and correctly because ventriloquists among the ancients, commonly abused the art of inward speaking for magical purposes. How then could it be that the same Hebrew word should express a bottle, and a ventriloquist: Apparently from the magician, when the possessed with the demon being as it were, a bottle or vessel, and sheath of this python (Acts 16:16)."

Thus, we get the teaching from these two words that the individuals who are telling the future or acting as mediums are doing so through demons. The demon is Python is named and appropriately so after Satan the snake and dragon himself. Python no doubt is a powerful demon over sorcery.

Biblical names for evil spirits

The Bible also names other evil spirits, and sometimes it is God that sends them. These are as follows:

- Spirit of whoredoms idolatry, adultery, fornication prostitution, false teachings (Hosea 4:12, 5:4)
- A lying spirit (1 Kings 22:22, 2 Chronicles 18:21-22)
- Spirit of Jealousy (Numbers 5:14, 5:30)
- An evil spirit (1 Samuel 16:14 Judges 9:23, Acts 19:16)
- Spirit of ill will Judges 9:23
- The evil spirit from God came upon Saul (1 Sa 18:10)
- Evil spirits (Luke 7:21, 8:2, Acts 19:12-13)
- Seducing Spirits (1 Titus 4:1)
- Spirit of deep sleep (Isaiah 29:10)
- Spirit of heaviness (Isaiah 61:3)
- Spirit of an Unclean devil (Luke 4:33)
- Spirit of infirmity (Luke 13:11)

- Spirit of the world (1 Corinthians 2:14)
- Spirit of Fear (2 Timothy 1:7)
- Spirit of Error (1 John 4:6)
- Unclean Spirit (immoral) (Matthew 12:43, Mark 1:26, 5:2, 5:8, 7:25, Luke 8:29, 11:24)
- Unclean spirits (Mat 10:1, Mar 1:27, Luke 6:18, Acts 5:16, 8:7)
- Other spirits more wicked (Matthew 12:45, Mark 3:1, 5:13, 6:7, Luke 4:36)
- He taketh seven other spirits more wicked than himself (Luke 11:26)
- Dumb spirit (Mark 9:17) could not speak
- Foul spirit (Mark 9:25) in conjunction with deaf and dumb spirit, (Revelation 18:2)
- Deaf and dumb spirit (Mark 9:25) Jesus cast this one out
- The spirits (Luke 10:20),
- Spirits of devils working miracles (Revelation 16:14)

While some of the Scriptures name several spirits such as jealousy, fear and depression and heaviness; there were others that caused sickness. The Bible mentions a spirit that triggers one to believe a lie and a host of unclean and evil spirits. The unclean lead people into all kinds of immorality. From these, we discover that there are hierarchies of angels and demons.

Strongholds

Strongholds are headed by a chief demon or archangel. In addition, clusters of demons build strong holds. These can exist over a building or home. In a person, you can have a demon and various spirits, having a stronghold on a person's life. There are also varying degrees of fortifications. The Bible provides an example of when more than one spirit enters a person, Mary Magdalene had seven. Luke 11:26 mentions that a spirit once cast out brings seven more along with him to enter the person. There was also the demon who identified itself as Legion because there were many in the person (Mark 5:9, 5:15). These are strongholds in a person, but these just do not exist over people.

To give an example of a strong hold, one time I was driving with a friend to Long Island. We took a wrong turn. Immediately I felt a major demonic presence. I could sense it throughout the entire building and even on the grounds of where we parked. Later when I looked up the location, I discovered it was the site of Pilgrim Psychiatric Center: the world's largest mental hospital. Built in 1929, at its peak it housed nearly 14k psychiatric patients. It was known for both lobotomy's and electro-convulsive therapy.

Spiritual Counterpart to all that is physical

In the spiritual realm, there is an angelic or demonic realm to the physical. Thus, there are demons and angels over countries, cities, and towns. In Revelation 7:1, we learn angels are over the four corners of the earth. Concerning the Four Living Creatures Zechariah 6:5 states they are the four spirits of the heavens. The arch angel Michael is over Israel. We also see that people are assigned demons and angels. In Matthew 18:10 Jesus references the angels that overlook children. In contrast are those who are demon oppressed or possessed.

Within the Satanic hierarchy, of all the demonic beings, it is the Antichrist, who invokes the most fear. Understanding him entirely, he is also the most shocking.

The Antichrist Son of Satan

3 THE ANTICHRIST ENTITY

It was the apostle John in 1 John 2:18 who first named him Antichrist and stated, "and as you have heard the Antichrist is coming." Jesus directly spoke of the Antichrist once in the Gospels. He referred to the one coming in his own name who the Jews will accept. John stated, "and as you have heard." This indicates that Jesus discussed details of the Antichrist to the apostles who taught others. It also confirms the Antichrist as the son of Satan. Why would Jesus discuss the coming of a mere man? This explains why the early church fathers, who were disciples of John wrote about the Antichrist. They wondered if he would arrive in their lifetime.

According to Vines Expository Dictionary of the New Testament, "Antichrist can mean "against Christ" or "instead of Christ," or perhaps, combining the two, 'one who assuming the guise of Christ, opposes Christ" (Westcott)." The meaning of his name Antichrist in the Greek antichristos means the adversary of the Messiah.

It Should Come

John states in 1 John 2:22, that the Antichrist denies the Father and the Son. 1 John 4:3 mentions the Spirit of the Antichrist that it affirms is already in the world. In addition, it states, that "whereof you have heard that it should come." Meaning that it will make its appearance, arise, come forth, be established, become known and this relates to persons.

What is striking about this phrase is the reference to the spirit of Antichrist, that shall come, arrive on the scene in the body of a man. This also occurs in other translations The questions is what is it? It is written, "it shall come", this is as it refers to the Spirit or Demon that is the Antichrist.

The entity that comes as a man

Irenaeus was a disciple of Polycarp, who was directly under the tutelage of the Apostle John. Irenaeus, stated, "For he (Antichrist) being endued with all the power of the devil, shall come. Concentrating in himself all Satanic apostasy and setting aside idols to persuade (men) that he himself is God, raising up himself as the only idol.

Larry Harper's book, "The Antichrist," summarizes the writings of Irenaeus and his student Hippolytus. Harper stated that according to the early church fathers the Antichrist's appears as a man because he seeks to reign as king over mankind and desires to focus the worship of God on himself.

In addition Harper states, "The Antichrist will be a Jew, and will achieve his stated objectives by being accepted as the Christ, the messianic king of the Jews, taking his seat in the rebuilt temple in Jerusalem pretending to be God Himself, and thereby becoming the "abomination of desolation" spoken of by the prophet Daniel and mentioned also by Jesus." Along with the early church fathers writing of the Antichrist, through the ages, each generation followed in their path.

Antichrist as Jewish Messiah

Jesus's taught that while the Jews rejected Him, the one coming in his own name they will accept. Theologian Arthur Pink noted in his book on the Antichrist that the word used indicates he is also from the lineage of Abraham. Not only would the Antichrist be hailed as the Jewish Messiah but would identify himself as God on this earth. The Antichrist is the nemesis of the Lord Jesus Christ. His coming would precede the second coming of Jesus.

The Antichrist heads the Final World Empire During the Tribulation

The book of Revelation provides the details of the horrific plagues that God will unleash onto the earth during the Tribulation.

The Tribulation is a seven-year period these plagues will occur. Part of the earth's judgments happen through the Antichrist. From the forecasts we know that he will be a dictator who will head the final world empire.

The kingdom that the early church fathers referred to is the revived Roman empire. He leads it to its pinnacle of power. At the event Jesus predicted and called 'the abomination of desolation' is when the Antichrist proclaims himself as God. This is what the early church fathers referred to as setting his kingdom up here on earth.

The Scriptures detail the Antichrist's reign of terror. Due to his anti-God, anti-Christ policies, he is named the Antichrist. His reign ignites Armageddon's battle. (Is. 14:12; Ezek. 28:3-4).

The Unholy Trinity-666

The number six, translated from the New Testament Greek into English, means "vex," or "curse." Seven represents God's number of perfection. The triple six represents the unholy trinity. The unholy trinity are named in the Scriptures as "The Dragon," "The Beast," and "The False Prophet." The Devil acts as God. The Antichrist, whom Satanists call the son of Satan, mimics Jesus Christ. The False Prophet mocks God's Holy Spirit. The Bible predicts he will come onto the earth and perform miracles to get the masses to worship the Beast. The

Unholy Trinity is yet another area, which teaches a triad of Satanic entities, confirming that the Antichrist is not an ordinary man. In addition to being a separate entity from Satan.

Arthur W. Pink on the Antichrist

Theologian Author Pink wrote extensively on Biblical theology. He wrote a good deal on the Antichrist. I will quote him several time throughout this work. He provided valuable insights, including a great piece on the Antichrist as the actual son of Satan.

He wrote this excellent summary on the Trinity vs. the Unholy Trinity:

"Is there a Holy Trinity, then there is also an Evil Trinity (Rev.20:10. In this Trinity of Evil Satan himself is supreme, just as in the Blessed Trinity the Father is (governmentally) supreme: note that Satan is several times referred to as a father (John 8:44, etc.). Unto his son, the Antichrist, Satan gives his authority and power to represent and act for him (Rev.13:4) just as God the Son received "all power in heaven and earth" from His Father, and uses it for His glory. The Dragon (Satan) and the Beast (Antichrist) are accompanied by a third, the

False Prophet, and just as the third person in the Holy Trinity, the Spirit, bears witness to the person and work of Christ and glorifies Him, so shall the third person in the Evil Trinity bear witness to the person and work of the Antichrist and glorify him. (see Rev.13:11-14)."

The Three Spirits like Frogs

The three spirits described in the Revelation provides another area, which indicates the Antichrist is part demonic entity. Revelation 16:13 states, "And I saw three unclean spirits like frogs come out of the mouth of the dragon, and out of the mouth of the beast, and out of the mouth of the false prophet. These three spirits of Satan parallel the seven spirits of God." Jesus named them when He stated in John 10:8-10, "the thief comes to kill, steal and destroy." This refers to Satan and his mission. Thus, the three spirits of Satan are kill, steal and destroy. These are issued out of the mouths of the unholy trinity near the time of the end to draw all the world's armies to the battle of Armageddon.

The fact that the Antichrist issues one of these out of his mouth, indicates that as part of the unholy trinity he not just a mere man. He is an entity in a man's body. He is powerful enough in Satan's hierarchy to issue spirits. We can break this down further and name the spirit for each of the member of the unholy trinity:

- Satan- the Dragon-Kill
- Antichrist- The Beast-Destroy
- False Prophet- False Teachings-Steal

The Beast

In Revelation 13 the beast of Revelation is described as rising out of the sea. It has ten horns and seven heads. It also represents the Antichrist. In the book, Jesus refers to the Antichrist by the name "the beast." This is significant because nowhere in Scripture is a man referred to in this way. This Beast reference is how God views this creature. Non-human, monstrous, an evil entity that seeks to bring glory to none other than Satan himself.

Arthur Pink notes the comparison of Jesus as the lamb, and the Antichrist as the Beast, possessing all manner of evil in part because he is not fully human.

The Scripture views the Antichrist as one with the government and empire. Would Adolph

Hitler exist the same in our minds without the Third Reich. Nero without the Roman Empire? Pol Pot without the Khmer Rouge? Therefore, the Beast's empire is clearly Satan's and one with the Antichrist. The Bible tells us that the various heads represent the world empires that have ruled Israel. The names of blasphemy are those kings who equated themselves with the gods. The Antichrist will declare that he is God.

Revelation 4 and Ezekiel 1 relay the description of the four living creatures. These are amidst the seven spirits of God. We see a depiction of their faces like a lion, calf, eagle, and man. The wording bears a similarity to the beast of Revelation. Whereas the Beast, with a mouth of a lion, body of a leopard and feet of a bear is amidst the three spirits of Satan. It is part of the dragon.

From this depiction we see that Satan has gone to considerable lengths to oppose God and mimic Him.

The Scarlet Red Dragon

In Revelation 12, the Beast with seven heads and ten horns is described as a fiery red dragon.

The dragon is Satan. Red in the Bible is the color of sin.

Revelation 13's monstrous description of the Beast given in Revelation 13, pairs with the book of Daniels. Daniel adds that it is extremely dreadful and strong: stamping the residue with its feet. Daniel also provides additional horrific details such as iron teeth and legs. Revelation 12 adds its appearance in its entirety as a red dragon.

Reference to Pharaoh king of Egypt

Only in one other area in Scripture do we have a reference to another monstrous king and that is in Ezekiel 29 2-3. It states, "Son of man, set your face against Pharaoh king of Egypt, and prophesy against him and against all of Egypt. Speak and say, 'Thus says the Lord God: "Behold, I am against you, O Pharaoh king of Egypt, O great monster who lies in the midst of his rivers, Who has said, 'My River is my own;'

This lines with the heads of blasphemy on the Beast. We know that the first head is Egypt. The monstrous beast in the sea is part of the Beast of Revelation, only in its earlier stage.

But, while the six initial kings were men who headed empires, the seventh and the eighth, which is of the seven, is the supernatural Antichrist.

666-The Number for a Name

Another area we see in Scripture evidence of the Antichrist as a demonic entity is the fact that he has a number for a name. Revelation 13:18 states: "And that no man might buy or sell, save he that had the mark, or the name of the beast, or the number of his name."

What we learn about the beast's number is that it is also his name. Nowhere in Scripture is anyone named with a number. It appears as if this verse does not belong because of this fact. This is the only place in the Bible where a man is named a number and we must ask why?

When we look at why a number is given for the Antichrist's name, we discover a deeper, hidden Biblical truth. In addition to what this means for those living during the Tribulation under the Antichrist's reign. It is evident that the redeemed are given a name, in contrast to the damned that are numbered. In my book **Decoding 666**, an entire chapter elaborates on all the passages supporting this teaching.

666-From birth appointed to death

The reason the Antichrist has a number for a name is because he is the son of Satan and is appointed to eternal death from his birth. If he were a man it would be contrary to the Bible's message that all men and women can receive salvation.

This also drives home the importance of having your name written in Heaven that comes with the belief in the name of Jesus. In contrast those who take the mark of the beast are numbered. They receive the number of the name of the Antichrist. In addition, they number themselves for death. The death I am speaking of is the Lake of Fire, which is eternal damnation. Daniel 12:1-2 affirms "…And at that time your people shall be delivered, Every one who is found written in the book. And many of those who sleep in the dust of the earth shall awake. Some to everlasting life, some to shame and everlasting contempt.

Antichrist's Judgement-Lake of Fire

This is another indication, that the Antichrist is

not fully human and is an entity apart from Satan. Principalities and powers such as Death and Hades are thrown directly into the Lake of Fire, as well as each member of the unholy trinity. The Antichrist is appointed to death i.e. the Lake of Fire from his birth and is thrown in without experiencing physical death. Revelation 19: 19-21 records:

"And I saw the beast, the kings of the earth, and their armies, gathered together to make war against Him who sat on the horse and against His army. Then the beast was captured, and with him the false prophet who worked signs in his presence, by which he deceived those who received the mark of the beast and those who worshiped his image. These two were cast alive into the lake of fire burning with brimstone. And the rest were killed with the sword which proceeded from the mouth of Him who sat on the horse. And all the birds were filled with their flesh."

Antichrist's Judgement Differs from Man's

Revelation 20 provides another indication that the Antichrist is not fully human. He does not receive the same judgment as man. Another signifier in Scripture of the Antichrist being an entity is his capture at the return of Christ. Both would not occur if the Antichrist were a mere man.

We learn that the Tribulation Saints, or those martyred during the Tribulation will reign with Christ during the 1000-year millennial reign. Revelation 20:5 states, "But the rest of the dead did not live again until the thousand years were finished. This is the first resurrection." Keep in mind that the Antichrist and the False Prophet are already in the Lake of Fire.

After the millennial reign, Satan is thrown into the Lake of Fire and joins the Antichrist and False prophet. Revelation 20:10 states: "The devil, who deceived them, was cast into the lake of fire and brimstone where the beast and the false prophet are. And they will be tormented day and night forever and ever."

Man's Judgment

Revelation 20:11-15 records man's judgment. Notice the Antichrist is not judged like men and women at the Great White Throne Judgment. He is already burning in the Lake of Fire.

"Then I saw a great white throne and Him who sat on it, from whose face the earth and the heaven fled away. And there was found no place for them. And I saw the dead, small and great, standing before God, and books were opened. And another book was opened, which is the Book of Life. And the dead were judged according to their works, by the things which were written in the books."

Death and Hades

We see in Revelation 20 that Death and Hades, the key principalities under Satan go into the Lake of Fire after giving up the souls of men and women reserved for judgement. This explains why they do not go in sooner. They are only delayed because they hold the souls for judgement. Again, if the Antichrist were a man his soul would have gone to Death and Hades and he would be in line to be judged according to his works like all other men and women. Revelation 20-13-15 reads:

"The sea gave up the dead who were in it, and Death and Hades delivered up the dead who were in them. And they were judged, each one according to his works. Then Death and Hades were cast into the lake of fire. This is the second death. And anyone not found written in the Book of Life was cast into the lake of fire."

The Antichrist-7ᵗʰ to the 8ᵗʰ Head

The Tribulation comprises two distinct periods, which is divided from the Tribulation to the Great Tribulation. This is reaffirmed by the 7ᵗʰ and 8ᵗʰ head of Revelation 17 as depicting two separate times in the final world empire's reign. The 7ᵗʰ and 8ᵗʰ head show us the division of these two periods. This passage also confirms the Antichrist as half devil.

According to Revelation 13 the Antichrist receives a mortal head wound and comes back to life. Revelation 13:3 states, "And I saw one of his heads as if it had been mortally wounded, and his deadly wound was healed." Revelation 13:12 adds, "And he exercises all the authority of the first beast in his presence and causes the earth and those who dwell in it to worship the first beast, whose deadly wound was healed."

Zechariah provides details of the wound

Zechariah 11:17 elaborates on the physical damage from the mortal wound. It predicts:

"Woe to the worthless shepherd, who leaves the flock! A sword shall be against his arm And against his right eye; His arm shall completely wither. And his right eye shall be totally blinded."

At midway through the tribulation the Antichrist is killed, or appears to be murdered, and he comes back to life. In this he mimics the death and resurrection of Jesus Christ. The Greek verb sphazo, which describes the mortal wound means to slay slaughter, butcher, to put to death by violence, mortally wounded.

The 8th head-the Resurrected Antichrist

Revelation 17:9-12, it reads: "Here is the mind which has wisdom: The seven heads are seven mountains on which the woman sits. There are also seven kings. Five have fallen, one is, and the other has not yet come. And when he comes, he must continue a short time. The beast that was, and is not, is himself also the eighth, and is of the seven, and is going to perdition."

Satan Enters into Antichrist?

Some scholars hold to the possibility that when

the Antichrist is raised from the dead Satan enters him and he becomes the 8th head. This is based on the idea of Satan entering Judas Iscariot.

Revelation 13: 3 states: "And I saw one of his heads as if it had been mortally wounded, and his deadly wound was healed. And all the world marveled and followed the beast." What is key is the phrase in Revelation 17 verse 3, "as if it had." Other definitions for the same word in the Greek mean, as if it were, according as, in the same manner as. The New King James version uses the phrase, "wounded to death." It could mean as if it were wounded to death.

The Antichrist is not fully a man, he is a devil, part of the unholy trinity. While Satan cannot give life, it is possible that this entity being part man would be able to bring its body back to life. For a normal man the wound would be fatal. For the Antichrist as an archangel he has the power to regenerate the body he inhabits. Thus, creating this miracle or the allusion of one that the whole world wonders after.

The Eighth Head

The eighth head can signify a form of the

Antichrist after his resurrected self. While still in a human body, he is primarily entity. Or it can also be merely that the deception that the Antichrist displayed in the first half of the Tribulation is now gone. Once he resurrects and the Abomination of Desolation occurs the Antichrist reveals his true colors. In the first half of the Tribulation the Antichrist lies and deceives. Once he survives the fatal wound, he removes the mask. In addition, at this time he has brought the EU to its height of power.

Jesus warned the Jews at the time of the Abomination of Desolation. This is when the Antichrist stands in the Third Jewish Temple in the Holy of Holies. He also declares that he is god and places the Abomination that makes desolate. This begins the Great Tribulation or second half of the Tribulation. This act marks the beginning reign of the 8th head and a second phase in his empire. Again, this will occur once the Antichrist resurrects and has the world in awe over his coming back to life.

As The 8th Head Antichrist Destroys Whore of Babylon

In Daniel 11:36-27 it reads: "Then the king shall do according to his own will: he shall exalt and magnify himself above every god, shall speak blasphemies against the God of gods, and shall prosper till the wrath had been accomplished, for what has determined shall be done. He shall regard neither the God of his fathers nor the desire of women, nor regard any god; for he shall exalt himself above them all."

It is also while under the leadership of the 8th head that the Whore of Babylon is destroyed. This means that at that time all world religions and especially the Jewish and Christian religions will be annihilated along with their followers. This begins the predicted persecution of the church-the 1260 days-characteristic of the great tribulation.

Son of Perdition

In John 13:27, Judas was called by Jesus the son of perdition. In John 17:12 and in 2 Thessalonians 2:3 the Antichrist is referred to as the son of perdition.

The only time the phrase son of perdition is used is with Judas and the Antichrist. Arthur Pink theorized that Judas would be reincarnated. Some hold the belief that the

Antichrist is Judas Iscariot. In the book of Acts the Scripture talks of him going to his own place. Revelation 17:9-11 mentions that the beast "is going to perdition," and that it rises from the bottomless pit (Revelation 17:8.)

Two Separate Person's

The Antichrist and Judas are both sons of perdition and are two separate entities. John states in 1 John 2:8 that "the Antichrist is coming." If he had already walked the earth in the form of Judas, the apostles would not have made separate references for him. In addition, the disciples of John looked to see if the Antichrist was alive in their time. If he had already lived, they would have known this.

The lives of both the Antichrist and Judas relay two important parallels and contrasts. Of the 24 Elders, both the 12 Sons of Jacob, and the 12 Apostles, one of each would be replaced. In the Revelation there is no mention of the tribe of Dan because Antichrist rises from it. Manasseh replaces Dan in Revelation 7:6. Of the 12 Apostles, Matthias replaced Judas. Judas was a man whose evil allowed Satan to enter him. Whereas the Antichrist, is an entity or a devil in a man's body.

The Antichrist Son of Satan

4 THE BOTTOMLESS PIT & THE RESTRAINER

Revelation clearly states that the Antichrist rises from the bottomless pit. The bottomless pit is mentioned only in the book of Revelation. It is the place where the demon Apollyon (Destroyer) is held. In addition to the angels/demons who sinned by fornicating with women, (Genesis 6) which created the giants or Nephilim. It is also the place which holds the Antichrist until his time to ascend and later where Satan will be confined during the millennial reign of Christ.

Revelation 17:8 reads: "The beast that thou sawest was, and is not; and shall ascend out of the bottomless pit, and go into perdition: they that dwell on the earth shall wonder, whose names were not written in the book of life from the foundation of the world, when they behold, the beast that was, and is not, and yet is."

As part of the unholy trinity, the beast who was, means that he existed along with Satan and was one of the entity's that departed heaven at the fall.

Revelation 11:7 reads, "And when they shall have finished their testimony, the beast who ascendeth out of the bottomless pit shall make war against them, and shall overcome them, and kill them.

Satan's Senior Entity's-Former Archangels

Satan's highest principalities with the greatest powers are The Antichrist, The False Prophet, Death and Hades. In an earlier chapter I stated that the Antichrist was most likely a former arch angel. The Bible refers to the Antichrist as "profane wicked prince of Israel. "Ezekiel 21:25-27 states, "Now to you O, profane, wicked prince of Israel, whose day has come, whose iniquity shall end, thus says the Lord God: Remove the turban, and take off the crown, Nothing shall remain the same, Exalt the humble, and humble the exalted, Overthrown, overthrown, I will make it overthrown! It shall be no longer, Until He comes whose right it is, And I will give it to Him."

In Daniel 10:21 Michael the archangel is referred to as a prince. It could be that the above reference of the 'wicked profane prince of Israel' has the double meaning of one who is taking the position as ruler over Israel, but also as one of the fallen princes' or archangels. This means that the Antichrist is most likely an archangel that was sent to the bottomless pit.

The Spirit of Antichrist

1 John 4:3 states, "And every spirit that does not confess that Jesus Christ has come in the flesh is not of God. And this is the spirit of the Antichrist, which you have heard was coming, and is now already in the world."

This verse refers to the to the fallen archangel who was named Antichrist. But this angel must have been directly under Satan and had a connection to him. This angel or spirit named Antichrist was so evil it was sent to the bottomless pit to be guarded by the restrainer.

If let out sooner, he would have changed the course of history and God's plan. God would allow Satan to send him but at the time of the end, and for God's purpose as part of the judgments on mankind.

The Rise out of the Pit-Removal by the Restrainer

The restrainer of 2 Thessalonians has been a mystery verse that many have taught on and there are many views. Based on this information, the restrainer is clearly the angel who is guarding the Antichrist from rising out of the pit. 2 Thessalonians 2:7 states: "For the mystery of lawlessness is already at work; only He who now restrains will do so until He is taken out of the way. And then the lawless one will be revealed, whom the Lord will consume with the breath of His mouth and destroy with the brightness of His coming."

Restrained Demons

We know from the Scriptures that the angels who sinned in Genesis 6 are chained in hell. 2 Peter 2:4-5 confirms, "For if God did not spare the angels who sinned but cast them down to hell and delivered them into chains of darkness, to be reserved for judgment."

Apollyon and Satan in the Bottomless Pit

Apollyon is also secured in the pit. One of the Revelation plagues is that the angel with the key goes to earth and opens the pit and releases Apollyon and his demonic locusts. Only these do not eat vegetation, they sting humans. The pain from the sting is the same as being bit by a scorpion. People do not die from the sting but suffer horrific pain from the sting. The plague lasts five months.

Finally, Satan after the Tribulation, during the millennial reign of Christ is also thrown into the bottomless pit. He is chained, and a seal is put over him. In Revelation 23:3, we learn that the angel not only chains him but later lets him lose for the rebellion at the end of the millennial reign.

Identity of Restrainer

The angel with the key to the bottomless pit is the restrainer. He has control over the demonic strongholds or entities chained or imprisoned in the abyss.

Jude 1:6 records: "And the angels who did not keep their proper domain, but left their own abode, He has reserved in everlasting chains under darkness for the judgement of the great day."

In 2 Thessalonians 2:7 if we break down the verse from the original word, while the entire definition is not included, those that apply are listed below:

- He who now-This present
- Letteth holds back, detains, retains, restrains, hinder, to hold down
- Strong's records, "of some troublesome condition or circumstance by which one is held as if it were bound.
- Will let until- until
- He be taken-come to pass, be made, be done, arise, be fulfilled, to become, come into existence, begin to be, to arise, appear in history, be made be brought to pass, arise, come, be
- Taken out of- from, out of, preposition denoting origin of point, where motion proceeds. From out of, out from, froth from, Universally, or the place form

which; from a surrounding or enclosing place, from the interior of the way
- midst, from among, from middle, between, in the midst of, either in the middle of a room or the midst of those assembled

The restrainer is therefore the angel over the abyss who has kept the spirit of Antichrist, from being released before his time.

The Bottomless Pit-The Abyss

The word in the Greek for bottomless pit means, the Abyss, the pit, the immeasurable depth, a very deep gulf, or chasm in the lowest parts of the earth. According to an article that appeared in Live Science the earth's core is 1000 degrees hotter than previously theorized. They stated that the planet's central mass is as hot as the surface of the sun. Keep in mind that the Bible was written before the scientific discoveries of the composition of the earth's core. For the most part the core remains a mystery.

We do not know how this spiritual dungeon exists within the foundation, other than the

Biblical descriptions. Moreover, it is related to the earth's core and magnetic field.

The False Prophet-From the Earth

The False Prophet appears during the start of the middle of the Tribulation, or at least at that time he gets recognition. He is the third member of the unholy trinity. He acts as the unholy spirit.

Based on the reasons for the Antichrist being supernatural, or a Nephilim, we begin to see that the False Prophet is an entity as well. As part of the unholy trinity he is thrown into the lake of fire along with the Antichrist.

The Beast rises from the sea, indicating the Mediterranean Sea. Revelation 13: 11 states that the False prophet, has two horns like a lamb, yet speaks like a dragon. While the beast rises from the sea, the false prophet comes up out of the earth.

Out of the Earth Meaning

The only other reference in the Bible to demons coming out of the earth is in 1 Samuel. As Saul descended into sin and further away from God, he went to a medium. Saul had once made sorcery illegal. He went to the medium of Endor for her to bring up the prophet Samuel. 1 Samuel 28 records the story and in verse 13 we see that spirits are ascending out of the earth.

It reads, "And the king said unto her, Be not afraid: for what sawest though? And the woman said unto Saul, I saw gods ascending out of the earth. In verse 11, the woman asked, "Who shall I bring up for you?" Compare this to Revelation 13:11 which reads, "Then I saw another beast coming up out of the earth." Given the other details, this is not talking about an empire rising to power, but rather, a spirit that has come up out of the earth. Could this also be the abyss?

The False Prophet Performs Signs and Wonders

According to Revelation 13:12-18, the false carries out or exercises all the authority of the first beast. So, he is like his Vice President. He causes all on the earth to worship the beast. Revelation 13:13-14 states, "And he performs great signs, so that he even makes fire come down from heaven on the earth in the sight of men. And he deceives those who dwell on the earth by those signs, which he was granted to do in the sight of the beast, telling those who dwell on the earth to make an image to the beast who was wounded by the sword and lived."

Another indication that the false prophet is not an ordinary man is found in verse 15. "He was granted power to give breath to the image of the beast, that the image of the beast should both speak and cause as many as would not worship the image of the beat to be killed.

God would not grant this kind of power to a man. We know He allows Satan to perform miracles. Therefore, we can conclude that God also allows high ranking Satanic entities, such as demonic arch angels to work them as well.

We are never told the False prophet is a man

The false prophet is also a demonic entity. The Bible refers to him as "another beast." We are never told in Scripture that he is a man. He appears as a man. Some have theorized a pope. I have even said possibly a scientist. Could the false prophet be one of the demonic spirits that entered the magicians from Egypt, possibly?

The False Prophet might be the arch angel or Demon that is over all sorcery. Possibly the same spirit that directed Balaam.

At the same time as the deception of the false prophet, God provides His two witnesses to also perform miracles. These also arrive back from the past. Some have theorized Elijah and Enoch, or Elijah and Moses.

This is the period of the supernatural that will occur during the Tribulation. Jesus warned of the false Christs and prophets who will perform signs and wonders. So great are the signs that Jesus said that if possible they can deceive the very elect (Matthew 24:24.)

Jesus might have even been referring to the False Prophet in this reference. Unlike the Antichrist who will be born, the False prophet seems to appear on the scene.

We do not know how long he exists along with the Antichrist before both come into power. The false prophet comes out of the earth, where Hades and the Abyss are located.

The Damnable Conception

The Bible does not tell us certain facts but gives enough information to connect the dots. When the restrainer releases the Antichrist or gets out of the way so the Antichrist spirit can depart, he will seek out a woman. He along with Satan will create conception within her body and from conception the Antichrist entity will indwell the woman's womb and become the spirit of the child.

The child will not have a God given soul that creates genuine life, but rather from its inception an entity indwells its human body. Imagine a human with no soul. The son of Satan, half devil, half man. This explains the Antichrist having a number for a name and referenced as 666 from birth. God allows Satan to perform this act. He allows the spirit of Antichrist to enter the conceived child versus a soul He creates.

The woman will not just be any woman. She will be Jewish and from the tribe of Dan. In the next section, we will look at the reason for the tribe of Dan, and its affiliation with Satan. Moreover as we investigate the tribe of Dan further in Scripture, we see the many indirect references to the Antichrist being born of a woman as well as of his being indwelled with a Devil and not just any Devil, but one that is the highest principality under Satan himself.

5 TRIBE OF DAN AND SATAN

In Genesis 3:16 is the Bible's first prophecy. It initiates the battle of the ages between God and Satan. It states, "And I will put enmity between you and woman, And between your seed and her Seed: He shall bruise your head And you shall bruise His heel."

Thy Seed and Her Seed

This verse has a duel meaning. It references man after the fall as having the devil as their father due to the DNA change and sin nature. From this time forward man would be born sinful and would have to make a willful decision to seek the true God.

As was stated in an earlier chapter, the knowledge of good and evil and the tree of life are DNA changing trees. Satan changed man's DNA so that physically his/her body would experience disease and then death. In addition to spiritual death.

The seed of woman represents the virgin birth. Satan's seed depicts all of mankind after the fall. This explains the reason why a new birth in Christ is essential for eternal life. This passage can also have a very literal meaning as well. The woman's seed is Christ representing the virgin birth. Satan's seed is his actual seed via intercourse with a woman. Her seed is Jesus, and his seed is the Antichrist. When God predicted this in the Garden, he already knew Satan's plan. Satan also realized that if he were to get man to fall in the Garden, that God would send His son Jesus to make reconciliation for the sin. At this early time the Spirit of Antichrist or the Entity that Satan entrusted would be given the task to counter the Christ.

Leviticus 66 days

According to Leviticus 12:1-8, if a woman bore a male child, the days of her purifying in which she could not touch anything holy or go into the sanctuary, were thirty-three days. In addition, she was unclean one week or seven days. One week is also the duration of the Tribulation to bring in holiness. Thirty-three years is the lifetime of Jesus. But, if she bore a female child, she was unclean fourteen or double the amount of days. She would continue in the blood of her purifying for 66 days.

Leviticus 12: 5 states, "But if she bears a female child, then she shall be unclean two weeks, as in her menstruation. And she shall continue in the blood of her purifying for sixty-six days.
At the end of these days she was to bring a lamb to the priest at the entrance to the tent of meeting. This of course represents the atonement of Christ. This is another area we see the contrast of Jesus to the Antichrist. The woman becomes the potential mate for Satan and thus the 66 days. In addition, a real male child is not produced, meaning one with a soul. But rather a demonic entity in a human body from birth.

Death and Hades

It was also at the fall that Death and Hades,

Satan's two chief principalities under the Unholy Trinity were given their task. Death would take the unredeemed souls and they would go to Hades.

In 1 Corinthians 15:53-55, the idea that the corruptible body must now put on incorruption to conquer Death and Hades is relayed, it reads, "For this corruptible must put on incorruption, and this mortal must put on immortality. So when this corruptible has put on incorruption, and this mortal has put on immortality, then shall be brought to pass the saying that is written: "Death is swallowed up in victory." "O Death, where is your sting? O Hades, where is your victory?" This verse talks directly to the principalities Death and Hades. The way to conquer them is through faith in Christ.

You Shall Bruise His Heel

The reference to the heel is also the first that relates the Antichrist to the tribe of Dan. But also the prediction that Christ shall crush the head of Satan. This also corresponds to Psalm 91:13, which represents Satan and the Antichrist. It reads, "You shall tread on the lion and the cobra, The young lion and serpent you shall trample underfoot. Another great illustration of this is in Isaiah 27:1, which states, "In that day the LORD with his sore and great and strong sword shall punish leviathan the piercing serpent even leviathan that crooked serpent; and he shall slay the dragon that is in the sea. This relates to the red dragon like beast that rises out of the sea of Revelation 13 with seven heads and ten horns.

The Lion of the Tribe of Judah-Redeemer

In Jacob's last words to his sons he also predicted their future. Jacob named Judah the kingdom line. From here we have what Scholars refer to as the lion of the tribe of Judah because Jacob called Judah a lion's whelp-a pride lion:

"Judah, you are he whom your brothers shall praise; Your hand shall be on the neck of your enemies; Your father's children shall bow down before you. Judah is a lion's whelp; From the prey, my son, you have gone up. He bows down, he lies down as a lion; And as a lion, who shall rouse him? The scepter shall not depart from Judah, Nor a lawgiver from between his feet, Until Shiloh comes.

Dan-Serpent by the Way

In addition, we see clearly that Dan matches the Garden account. He is a serpent by the way, and he bites the horse's heels, which we can reference back to bruising Christ's heel. The passage reads: "Dan shall judge his people As one of the tribes of Israel. Dan shall be a serpent by the way, A viper by the path, that bites the horses heels so that its rider shall fall backward."

Genesis 49: 17 continues, "Dan shall be a serpent by the way and adder in the path that bites the horse's heels so that its rider shall fall backward." When we think of the serpent, we think of the Devil who tempted Eve. Dan is a type of Devil whose idolatrous ways will influence the rest of the tribes of Israel in having them fall backwards into idolatry and its lies vs. their allegiance to the God of Israel. This is Satan's work in Israel and through the ages among the Gentiles.

Dan Shall Judge His People

According to Jacob, Dan will come to judge his people. The word used for judge means to act as a judge, minister judgment, requite, vindicate, govern, contend, strive, to be at strife, quarrel. Dan will judge his people meaning that the Antichrist will come from the tribe of Dan and will cause them the greatest hardship by acting as a judge for his people causing their judgment.

Jeremiah 8:16, which prophesizes about the last days states, "The snorting of his horses was heard from Dan. The whole land trembled at the sound of the neighing of his strong ones: For they have come and devoured the land and all that is in it, the city and those who dwell in it." In the same context Chapter 17 continues, "For behold I will send serpents among you, Vipers which cannot be charmed. And they shall bite you, says the Lord." This is the fulfillment back to the prediction that Dan will judge his people and his being a serpent by the way and is talking about the Antichrist's siege of Israel during the Tribulation.

Dan Associated with Idolatry

Why Dan? To understand why Dan, we must look at the tribe's origin. Rachel, the wife of Jacob was both beautiful and like most Biblical patriarchs had her area of sin. Rachel could not have any children. She became jealous of her sister Leah who bore Jacob four sons while she sat childless. She became angry at Jacob and blamed him for her barren state. In Rachel's envy she grabbed her maid Bilhah and gave her to Jacob as a surrogate to have children for her. Bilhah bore Dan. Jealous rivalry continued between Rachel and Leah. Rachel's maid bore a second son to her: Naphtali.

Rachel's Idolatry

When Jacob left the home of his father in law, Rachel stole his idols. She lied to her father as he searched for them so that he would not find them. She also kept this secret from her husband Jacob. He did not know that she had stolen the idols from her father. Rachel's attachment to the idols was so great that she stole them. In addition, she lied to protect them. Although Dan was born by Rachel's concubine, Bilhah, Rachel mothered him. He followed her in her idolatry.

Micah's Idol

Judges Chapters 17 and 18 tells the story of Micah an idolater who lived in the mountains of Ephraim. He employed a renegade, idolatrous priest. Dan and 600 of his men went searching the land for an area to settle. They came upon Micah's house. They forcibly took his idols and his priest to serve them. The Danites then went into Laish. They took the land by murdering its inhabitants. They renamed it Dan. The Tribe of Dan set up Micah's idol. In addition, they employed idolatrous priests to serve them until their captivity.

In summary Dan went into the home of Micah, stole his idols and his pagan priest. They went with 600 men. Here again is the number six. They went into the peaceful village of Laish, which had no king. The Danites proceeded to murder all the inhabitants and set the village on fire before taking it over. Dan had been given a coastal portion of land. Yet, they went as far north as they could possibly go and established the City of Dan. They removed themselves to the farthest end of the nation, while still being part of it. Afterwards the Bible referred to Israel as from Dan to Beersheba.

Currency and Idolatry

Dan set up idolatry in defiance of Israel's God. In Scripture currency is synonymous with idolatry. In Judges chapter 17, we learn of the image of Micah that was made from money that his mother saved. She did so for the purpose of making it into an idol. It ended up in Micah's shrine. He made his own son a priest. In addition, he employed a renegade Levitical priest.

The Danites went to seek an inheritance for themselves of land, Judges 17:18 records, "for until that day their inheritance among the tribes of Israel had not fallen to them." In searching the land they went to the home of Micah and recognized his idolatrous priest. They went to peaceful Laish, killed the inhabitants, and burned the city. Upon taking over the land and rebuilding it they named it Dan. Afterwards they went to Micah's home, took his idols and his priest to serve the entire tribe.

The Danites were given land on the coast but Israel's northern kingdom's first king was King Jeroboam. The Bible mentions over and over that he is "the man who caused Israel to sin." He placed two golden calves, which he set up for idolatrous worship. Jeroboam placed one in Bethel and the other in Dan. These both lay on the extreme southern and northern part of the kingdom (I Kings 29-30). Bethel afterwards became a center for idolatry. Dan already existed as one, which is why Jeroboam placed a calf there.

In Amos 8:14 which foretells Israel's captivity, God declares judgment on Dan for its allegiance to its false gods. It states, "Those who swear by the sin of Samaria, Who say, "As your god lives, O Dan! And, 'As the way of Beersheba lives! They shall fall and never rise again."

Dan Omitted from Revelation 7

While the tribe of Dan was known for idolatry, the tribe is also noted for Samson, and skilled workers for Solomon's temple. Also considered experts in war the Danites supported David who was king of Judah in becoming king of a re-united Israel.

Never-the-less The Bible well establishes the idolatry of the tribe of Dan. This is one reason it is not mentioned among the 12 tribes in Revelation chapter 7. It also explains why Dan provides the Antichrist's lineage. The Antichrist sets himself up as a god in the Jewish Temple. The false prophet causes the world to worship it. The Antichrist commits the ultimate idolatry and abomination.

Dan Seafarers Associated with King of Tyre

At the time of Judges, the Danites were also known as seafarers. Dan was given a small strip of land on the coast, where they became mariners. In the song of Deborah in Judges 5:17, Deborah references the Danites as remaining on their ships. Dan in its early history is also associated with Tyre. The Phoenicians were also seafarers. Tyre (which is now Lebanon) was a major Mediterranean seaport from about 2000 BCE through the Roman Empire.

King of Tyre

Tyre is a coastal city, in ancient times it was known for the beautiful purple dye derived from shells on its coast. The Bible even references its purple dye. Hiram King of Tyre grew Tyre into a large trading empire. In the kingdom period of Israel, David and Solomon held close relations with Tyre. Hiram, a Phoenician king of Tyre supplied Solomon men and building materials for the building of the Temple.

It was Hiram of Tyre who expanded trade. He brought in gold from Ophir along with peacocks, and sandalwood and other items. The alliance of Hiram and Israel facilitated and expanded trade through trade routes to Egypt, Arabia, and Mesopotamia.

During this period, the Tribe of Dan intermarried with the Tyrians. This is evidenced in 2 Chronicles 2:14 which states, "The son of a woman of the daughters of Dan, and his father was a man of Tyre, skillful to work in gold and in silver, in brass, in iron, in stone, and in timber, in purples, in blue, and in fine linen, and in crimson, and to grave any manner of graving, and to find out every device which shall be put to him, with thy cunning men, and with the cunning men of my lord David, thy father."

This lends to why the Danites were also known for being metal craftsman. From the above list, wood and fabric were included in addition to metals. While the skills were utilized in Solomon's temple, they would also be used for the making of the idols of the Danites and the Phoenicians.

Based on the Scriptures the Danites now

inhabited two locations, yet they still were a united tribe of Israel.

King of Tyre is Satan

The pairing of the Danites and Phoenicians of Tyre lends another hint of supernatural Antichrist. The Bible equates the King of Tyre with Satan. For one of the descriptions of Satan, we read in Ezekiel 28 the passage of the King of Tyre. God viewed this king as Satan's equivalent.

While the Bible does not name the exact King of Tyre, he was possibly Ithobaal 1. He died in 847 BC. Originally, he was a priest of the goddess Astarte, a form of Ishtar of Babylon. He also worshipped Baal as his name evidences. He founded a new dynasty. During his reign Tyre expanded its power and territory.

Jezebel

Ithobaal's daughter was Jezebel. She became the wife of Israel's King Ahab. Her evil deeds are even spoken of by Jesus in the Revelation. She was responsible for Baal becoming the primary god in Israel. Elijah challenged 400 of her prophets and after winning killed them all.

Jezebel then sought to kill Elijah.

Jezebel in the Bible represents total evil personified in a woman. It is no surprise she is the daughter of the King of Tyre who equates to Satan. In addition, the Antichrist rises from the Tribe of Dan, and we see that early in their history, their bloodline is mingled with the descendants of the King of Tyre, which includes Jezebel.

6 LION OF BASHAN - NEPHILIM

Moses Blessing to the 12 Tribes Names Bashan

Moses before he died, provided another blessing or poem as did Jacob. Only we have additional details for both Dan and Judah. This is recorded in Deuteronomy Chapter 33. Moses's blessing speaks of Judah as presented or brought to his people. Moses references Dan as a lion's welp like Judah in Jacob's blessing, but also as a lion who leaps from Bashan.

Deuteronomy 33:7 records, "And this he said of Judah: "Hear, Lord, the voice of Judah, And bring him to his people;

Let his hands be sufficient for him, And may You be a help against his enemies."

And of Dan Deuteronomy 33:22 records he said: "Dan is a lion's whelp; He shall leap from Bashan."

Lion of Bashan is in Attack Mode

We see in the passage that like Judah as "a lion's whelp" recorded in Genesis 49:9, a lion's whelp also represents Dan. but instead of the pride lion that represents Judah, this is the scavenger lion. This pride kicks this lion out and he wanders as a nomad seeking who he may devour (1 Peter 5:8). This lion leaps from Bashan.

The word in the Hebrew for leap means that this lion is about to dart on his prey. The lion of Bashan is in hunting mode. He has his prey well in his sites and springs into the attack. The depiction of the lion about to pounce its prey describes Dan's brutal attack on the peaceful Phoenician city of Laish. In addition, to the Danites known as experts in warfare and area the Antichrist will also be skilled. Moreover describing the Antichrist's future attacks.

The Antichrist Depicted as a Lion in the books of Daniel and Revelation

Throughout the books of Daniel and the Revelation, we see the image of the lion of Bashan in describing the Antichrist. In both books we see that the Beast or the Antichrist has the mouth of a lion.

Revelation 13:2 states: "And his mouth as the mouth of a lion." Daniel 7:4 adds, "The first was like a lion and had eagles wings." This represents Babylon, which symbolizes the first head on the Beast of Revelation. Bible Scholars consider the King of Babylon as another title for the Antichrist and a forerunner of him.

The lion's den of the book of Daniel represents the Antichrist's government. Those who do not take the mark of the beast will find themselves in the lion's den i.e. the prisons of the Antichrist's police state. The book of Daniel exists as a future book written for the Tribulation Saint's

Lion of Tribe of Judah Vs. Lion of Bashan

The lion of Bashan acts as the nemesis of the lion of the tribe of Judah. The reason for the conflict and battle of the ages? Satan created by God as the highest angel, wanted to be like God. He considered himself like the Son of God.

In Jacob's blessing to his 12 sons, Judah is established as royal lineage of the King of Kings. Dan is of the snake in the garden, that will bite the heels. The reference and prediction that is in Genesis 2, is that Satan will bruise Christ's heel, but Jesus Christ will crush its head.

In Moses's blessing you have the Christ presented to his people and the Antichrist as leaping in an attack.

In summary Jesus rises from the tribe of Judah and the Antichrist from the tribe of Dan. Both Jesus and the Antichrist are symbolized by lions. Jesus is the pride lion and the Antichrist the scavenger lion. Both Jesus and Dan are referred to as a "lion's whelp" in Scripture. But the lion of Bashan is not an ordinary lion.

The Kings of Bashan as types of Antichrist

In the Bible there are two kings who ruled Bashan and each of these kings is a representation of the Antichrist. They provide more details of why the Lion of Bashan is a depiction of the Antichrist.

Og of Bashan -a giant

Og according to the Hebrew Bible, was an Amorite king of Bashan who, along with his army, was slain by Moses and his men at the battle of Edrei. What is significant is that Og was a giant.

Deuteronomy 3:11-12 tells us that Og was a remnant of the giants and provides the enormous size of his bed. It was 14 feet by 6 feet in width. The passage reads: "For only Og king of Bashan remained of the remnant of the giants. Indeed, his bedstead was an iron bedstead. (Is it not in Rabbah of the people of Ammon?) Nine cubits is its length and four cubits its width, according to the standard cubit."

Further down in verse 13 Bashan was referred to as the land of giants. It reads, "And the rest of Gilead, and all Bashan, being the kingdom of Og, gave I to the half tribe of Manasseh; all the region of Argob, with all Bashan, which was called the land of giants.

Og was a Nephilim

Og was a Nephilim. The Nephilim are recorded in Genesis 6:1-6, which states:

"Now it came to pass, when men began to multiply on the face of the earth, and daughters were born to them, that the sons of God saw the daughters of men, that they were beautiful; and they took wives for themselves of all whom they chose. And the Lord said, "My Spirit shall not strive with man forever, for he is indeed flesh; yet his days shall be one hundred and twenty years." There were giants on the earth in those days, and also afterward, when the sons of God came in to the daughters of men and they bore children to them. Those were the mighty men who were of old, men of renown."

The Nephilim or giants were created by evil angels. These were punished by God and are now locked away in chains in the Abyss. This was discussed in an earlier chapter.

It should also be noted that stories of ancient Sumerian gods bear similar stories to the Nephilim in their own mythology.

The Nephilim were not killed off in the Flood

Some Bible Scholars teach that the Nephilim were killed off in the flood. But we see Nephilim leaders who were fought by both Moses and Joshua and defeated. Nephilim did exist after the flood.

Astronomer Dr. Hugh Ross provides the best explanation on his blog *Reasons to Believe, How did the Nephilim appear after the Flood,* He states:

"The explanation for the post-flood Nephilim is that sons of God, distinct from those who went to the daughters of humans before the flood, went to the daughters of humans born after the flood. If these sons of God were fallen angels, then these fallen angels are in addition to the ones who were locked up in the abyss because of their having sexual relations with human females before the flood.

Thus, the abyss would contain two sets of fallen angels: those who had violated human women before the flood and those who had violated human women after the flood. ... Thanks to a small Hebrew nation, and especially to David and his mighty men, the few post-flood Nephilim were completely exterminated."

Og's Kingdom Discovered and Provided Evidence of Land of Giants

Og of Bashan was a Nephilim. While it sounds as if it is a fairy tale for the Nephilim to have existed, Josias Leslie Porter an Irish Presbyterian minister, missionary and traveler who lived between 1823 and 1889 discovered evidence of giants. Porter wrote for Smith's Bible Dictionary and the Encyclopedia Britannica among other notable works. He wrote in his book, "The Giant Cities of Bashan and Syria's Holy Places that the dimensions of the massive building's archways and ceilings evidenced a land of giants that the Bible described. This includes Og of Bashan's palace. Og was considered a famous and great king according to Psalm 136:20.

Biblical Significance of Giants

Og was defeated as were the other giants, which also included Goliath, the Philistine that David slew with his sling shot. Giants are always depicted as the most frightening enemies of Israel that inhabit the land. In the book of Joshua, we see the formula for getting rid of these enemies is always obedience and reliance on the God of the Bible. God's power easily defeats the giants.

The Nephilim Giants-Agents of Satan

The giant's association with the Nephilim relays their demonic character. They are formidable foes that can crush and destroy their opponent. Satan's task is to come, steal, kill and destroy. His demonic hordes are given the task. Many have been annihilated under his hand. His demons crush them to the point of death. It will be with the Antichrist and his dictatorship.

From Bashan we see the association with the Nephilim: Satan's demons who mated with women. Og the giant was one of the offspring. Og from Bashan is a type of Antichrist. He was defeated by God.

What is noteworthy about Og of Bashan is it is the first Antichrist type in the Bible where we see a direct association with demons cohabitating with women. Thus, the lion of Bashan is a demonic lion.

Scholars have not been able to figure out why the Danites were associated with Bashan or a lion from the city when their history had nothing to do with the area. They missed the s link relayed to you in this book.

Bashan and its Association with Satan

In many areas in Scripture when Bashan is used, it somehow relates to Satan and the Antichrist. Hazael an evil king who defeated the Kings of Israel both King Jehoram of Israel and King Ahaziah of Judah. He made the prophet Elisha weep. In 2 Kings 8:7-14 we learn Elisha wept as he told Hazael that he would become king. This is because Elisha knew all the evil atrocities that Hazael would commit against the children of Israel.

In 2 Kings 13 we learn that although Hazael oppressed Israel during the reign of Jehoahaz, God had compassion. After Hazael's death, King Jehoash the son of Jehoahaz recaptured from Hazael's son all the cities captured by Hazael. King Hazael is thought to have been born in Bashan. This evil king who committed such atrocities that he caused Elisha to weep while foretelling his reign, is another type of Antichrist.

Antichrist a type of Nephilim

The Antichrist is a type of Nephilim, meaning that he will be fathered by a demon, Satan himself facilitating the task along with the Spirit of Antichrist. The Antichrist like Jesus will appear as an ordinary man. Only he is without a soul.

We see in the land of the giants their supernatural and demonic aspect. This is the realm of Antichrist.

Bashan had 60 Cities

Another indicator for the Antichrist is the number 60. Bashan encompassed a small area of land and yet managed to have 60 cities within it. Sixty cities! Each city was fortified with walls.

We also see another six with the 600 men of Dan who went into Laish. The most significant 6 is the 666 of Revelation 13:18, which is the number of the name of the Antichrist. Of the multiples of 6 in the Bible, several relate directly to the tribe of Dan, to idolatry and to Og of Bashan and the giants.

Biblical Sixes and Nines Among the Nephilim.

Among the Nephilim we see varying 6's and this includes on the toes and fingers of the giant Goliath. 2 Samuel 21:20 records:
"Yet again there was war at Gath, where there was a man of great stature, who had six fingers on each hand and six toes on each foot, twenty-four in number and he was also born to a giant."

The number 9 is a number for wars

In Deuteronomy we learned that Bashan's bedstead was 9 feet and 4 feet wide. Nine is the number of war. If you add them both together you get the number 13. Deuteronomy 3:11, affirms, "For only Og of Bashan remained of the remnant of the giants. Indeed his bedstead was an iron bedsted. (Is it not in Rabbah of the people of Ammon?) Nine cubits is its length and four cubits its width, according to the standard cubit."

Nephilim do not receive salvation

In the Old Testament all the Nephilim were

considered enemies and were killed. We do not read of one instance of one becoming righteous. Thus, we can conclude that salvation could not happen within the Nephilim. This supports the Antichrist as being given a number for a name. Meaning he is destined for hell from birth.

Jesus's reference to the bulls of Bashan

Finally, we see in the prophetic Psalm 22, Christ on the cross reference many bulls surrounding him. He mentions the "strong bulls of Bashan" as representing His enemies. One can only imagine that Satan and all his demons were around Jesus adding to His torment in addition to working through Judas, the Romans and all those who wanted Him dead.

With all of this in mind, the land of Bashan is a place of demonic hoards. The Lion of Bashan counterparts the Lion of the Tribe of Judah. One the Son of God, and the other the Son of Satan.

Og of Bashan Hints at Antichrist's birth

In addition, the fact that Og of Bashan was a

Nephilim, which offspring resulted from demons having sexual relations with women, provides another hint the Antichrist's birth will occur in the same manner. This lends to the Antichrist's supernatural ability to survive a fatal wound. It also explains the reason for the number of his name. This is Scripture's only reference of someone with a number for a name. This is because a demon will be involved in his conception. Furthermore, with the many contrasts that exist in Scripture between Christ and the Antichrist, the birth of the Antichrist becomes another.

Many Scriptures Point to the Antichrist as the son of Satan

As I illustrated in all the above passages, these all point to the Antichrist as the son or ambassador of Satan. He will essentially be a type of Nephilim. Part man, part entity. From the time of his birth be very connected to Satan. This is in part why the book of Daniel refers to the Antichrist as "vile." In addition to being called, the "profane wicked prince." It also explains why the Antichrist is captured and thrown into the Lake of Fire instantly after the Tribulation.

7 BIRTH-BLOODLINE OF ANTICHRIST

One can only wonder about the birth of the Antichrist. The story of Rosemary's baby, which was pure fiction, might have some truth to it. Would a woman steeped in Satanism be the candidate for the Antichrist's mother? Who would Satan choose to birth his son? Would the woman even know? We will never have these answers. The women who birthed the Nephilim were anonymous.

Montague Summers was an English author and questionable clergyman born in 1880 and died in 1948. He was considered an expert in witchcraft and the occult, based on his books on the topic. In his book, "The History of

Witchcraft and Demonology" published in 1926 he wrote concerning the Sabbat or Black Mass, that during its proceedings, "They give themselves up to every kind of filthy abomination. The Devil transforms himself into an Incubus and into a Succubus. The hideous orgies and foul copulations practiced by the Euchites and Gnostics.

The Bloodline of the Antichrist

Yet there is a specific bloodline for the Antichrist. While there is not a way to exactly trace it, we can follow it in more general terms. The Bible tells us two facts about the bloodline, the Antichrist rises from the tribe of Dan in Europe. Daniel 8:9-10 records, "And out of one of them came a little horn which grew exceedingly great toward the south, toward the east, and toward the Glorious Land. It grew up to the host of heaven; and it cast some of the host and some of the stars to the ground and trampled them."

According to Daniel Chapter 8, the little horn rises from one of the four horns of Alexander the Great's empire. When he died, his kingdom went to his generals. One presided over Macedon, which was later absorbed by the

Roman Empire. Daniel 9:27 predicts the prince who is to come will be the same people who will destroy the City and the sanctuary. This was the destruction of the second temple by the Romans in A.D. 70. Therefore, he will come from the Revived Roman Empire, which is now the European Union. The Antichrist will rise from a European Union nation.

Tribe of Dan Dispersion Recorded in 2 Kings

2 Kings 17:6 records the disbursement of the ten tribes under the Assyrian empire around 722 BC. The Assyrians relocated and dispersed those it conquered to prevent them from forming an army. 2 Kings 17:6 records: In the ninth year of Hoshea, the king of Assyria took Samaria and carried Israel away to Assyria, and placed them in Halah and by the Habor, the River of Gozan, and in the cities of the Medes.

The Jewish historian Josephus (37-100 CE) wrote that "the ten tribes are beyond the Euphrates till now and are an immense multitude and not to be estimated in numbers." The Danites migrated to Greece and to Marseilles and through Europe upwards to

Ireland and Denmark. This migration began before the dispersion.

The bloodline for the Antichrist is shown in the Beast of Revelation depiction.

The beast of Revelation is a red scarlet beast that has seven to eight heads with the names of blasphemy. On one of the heads are ten horns. These are the kingdoms that align with the Antichrist during the Tribulation.

The Revelation depiction begins with Satan as the Dragon. It goes from the empires or kingdoms of Egypt to Babylon, Medo Persia, Greece and Rome. The seventh and eighth heads comprise of Revived Rome during the Tribulation. On each of the heads of the beast are the names of blasphemy. This is because those kings took on the names of the gods or named themselves sons of the gods. Not to mention Satan is in control of the kingdoms of this world. In addition, the Bible clearly states that demons are in the gods.

Eight Heads and the names of blasphemy

- Egypt-Pharaoh- god-ra-the good god, the good shepherd

- Assyria-King-god Asher-son of god, father of gods
- Babylon-King-god Marduk/Bel (lord)-god, my son of god
- Medo Persia-god Ahura Mazda-King-king of kings, king of the world
- Greece-King- god Zues-son of god
- Rome during early Roman Empire-Emperor-god, All of above-deliverer, savior god on earth
- Rome during Tribulation's first half-President-god-Antichrist
- Rome During Tribulation's second half. -President-god-Antichrist

The gods of the ancients go by different names, yet all relate. Like today there were worldwide religions, with varying sects. They were called differant titles based on the god of their religion and region. This includes Tyre, which is not represented by one of the heads, but who's king the Bible relates to Satan himself. As the tribe of Dan mingled with the Phoenicians and aligned with them, they adopted their gods.

Tyre-The following gods are the same Melqart of Tyre to Hercules of Greece.

These gods are also the same and come from a variety of lands including Tyre. Zeus, Marduk, Dagon, Dyaus, Daonos, Daos, Deus Diu-Peter, and Jupiter.

The Babylonian/Akkadian Marduk was also known under the name "Bel", which equates with "Baal" The sea peoples carried the idea of Baal/Bel to the British Isles, where he was known as "Belenus." Celts celebrated his festival, known as "Beltane", on May 1."

The Phoenicians colonized the Mediterranean from 1200 to 800 BCE. From their presence came the story of the birth of Europe.

Europa was a Phoenician Princess, the daughter of Agenor, king of Tyre. She was walking along the seashore with her companions. She was noticed by Zeus who transformed himself into a white bill. When she went to sit on it, Zeus abducted her and rushed to the sea and took her to Crete, returned to his human appearance and raped Europa. Her three brothers, searched for her, and thus the birth of Europe occurred in mythology.

The Dragon Bloodline

The late Prince Nicholas de Vere von Drakenbert wrote the Dragon Legacy. According to his biography, "His family's hereditary involvement in royal witchcraft and the Dragon tradition was recognized by the Black Country Covenant of the Baphometic Order of the Cubic Stone.

He was bestowed with the highest accolade of the covenant: that of Magister Templi. The Order traced its origins back to the Knights Templars and Nicholas was able to use his investiture as an invocational key in the pursuit of deeper, unwritten knowledge." In an article he described the various kingdoms beginning with Assyria. He wrote of the Annunnaki, including the gods breeding with the Nephilim. From there he describes the dragon symbolism from kingdom to kingdom.

The similarity of the Biblical story with the mythological could easily have resulted from the ancient Jewish history of their adopting the gods of their neighbors. In addition, the demons are in the gods, which means that there is also a demonic influence in these similar stories.

Conspiracy Teachings-13 Satanic Bloodlines

There are false teachers who have written on the 13th Satanic bloodlines and bloodlines of the Illuminati. These are not only more conspiracy theories but rely on occult teachings instead of Bible and poorly connect the dots.

As many conspiracy theorists they site the Freemasons and Illuminati and even the Templars. They also trace the tribe of Dan to one country. Finally, they ended up with an identity of a person who is not even in politics. In one instance the person has since died. They were still convinced he was the Antichrist based on the bloodline.

Merovingian Line of Kings

Of all the bloodlines, the Merovingians pose the greatest possibility for the line Satan would choose.

According to the late Tracy R. Twyman, Who is the man we call Dagobert?

"Dagobert II was a French king from the sacred Merovingian bloodline, the last Merovingian to hold the title "New Constantine." The Merovingians were a dynasty of Frankish priest-kings who were believed by their subjects to have magical powers derived from their long hair. There were rumors of witchcraft, fortune telling and crystal-ball gazing being practiced among them. In fact, portraits of Merovingian kings customarily depict them holding one of these crystal balls in the left hand."

Sorcerer Kings

Essentially these kings were seers, like those recorded in the Biblical history of Egypt and Babylon. The sorcerers were likely in the tradition of the ones we saw in Egypt with Pharaoh at the time of Moses. These were able to accomplish serious feats and duplicate Aaron's miracles.

The Merovingian kings were known as the sorcerer kings. Since these early kings those in the ancestral line have testified of possessing various powers. They attribute these abilities to the dragon bloodline. But some believe that Jesus and Mary Magdalene married and had a child. And their speculated offspring lend to the powers. From here it goes into the grail legend and the power of various artifacts.

If Jesus had married, it would have negated His claims. On the powers, given that the Merovingians were seers and magicians, after the Egyptian and Babylonian tradition, this follows the Biblical bloodline illustration of the Scarlet Beast. The spirits that gave them the magical capabilities would transfer to each generation.
No doubt they are also lying spirits seeking to negate the power of Christ. This explains why the legend took a blasphemous turn for some. This is the teaching that Jesus and Mary Magdalene were married.

Simon the Sorcerer- Magician

Simon the sorcerer of Acts 8:9-24, which Irenaeus and other early church fathers described as the father of Gnosticism, was from a village named Gitta. According to Josephus, the town was settled by the tribe of Dan. Gittim has an association with Gath, which was one of the locations or last refuges of the Giants or Nephilim. Through this indirect reference we have an association with the Danites and sorcery.

The Merovingians and Danites

From the King of Tyre, to each of the heads on the Scarlet beast we see the various gods, are all in sync. In addition, their relation to the Tribe of Dan and the Merovingian Kings.

While we are not sure of how the tribe of Dan found its way into the royal bloodline, the symbols of the Danites are present. In the Frankish Merovingian kings, we see the long hair of Samson to the symbol of the bee. Although the bee also has occult meanings. Therefore, the bloodline is a possibility for the mother of the Antichrist.

The Merovingians originated in what today would be the countries of Western Europe. Their origin was with the Gaul's, who were Celtic people. There are scholars who write that the Celts were the Tribe of Dan. While we know that the Danites were throughout Europe, there is evidence that the Danites were in the heart of Europe and the very region of the Merovingian Kings: Alsace, France.

8 RISING FROM EUROPE

Evidence of the Tribe of Dan in Alsace France

Historian Count Christian d'Andlau Hombourg, a Merovingian descendant discovered evidence of the Tribe of Dan in the Alsace region of France. This is significant for two reasons. First it supports the Merovingians as having Danite blood. Second it places the Danites in central Europe. Thus, providing the potential of the Antichrist rising from more European nations: France, Germany, Belgium and Luxembourg.

Count Christian d'Andlau proves the tribe of Dan's mark on the medieval Catholic churches in Alsace: The Abbatial Church of Andlau and the Abbey Church of ST Richard. In addition to their relation to the Grail family, who are his ancestors He stated:

All the symbols of the tribe of Dan are there : the lion of Bashan jumping to the North ; the lion of Juda being killed by Samson ; the **Dan**aïdes ; the Spartans ; the legend of Dietrich von Bern (King Theodoric) travelling from Italy to **Dan**emark ; the eagle symbol chosen by Dan himself to replace the snake which had been attributed to him by Jacob ; the bears, symbols of king Arthur (from Artios, the bear divinity of fertility) ; and many symbols of the Grail saga ; etc, etc.

Along with the Danites embracing the Catholic faith, the symbols of their lineage and idolatry are there. This includes a depiction of a version of Poseidon riding a dolphin. This makes sense because the Danites were seafarers. With their close alliance with the Phoenicians (King of Tyre) they also adopted the worship of the sea gods. These include Melqart-son of Poseidon and Baal, son of the fish god Dagon. Melqart is depicted riding a sea horse.

It should also be noted that in these churches along with within the Vatican museum is evidence of the idolatry that accompanied the

Catholic faith. Catholicism merged the pagan religions which originated from Sumerians and Babylonians, Egyptians, and Greeks, with Catholicism.

I visited the churches with Count Christian d'Andlau Hombourg

Count Christian d'Andlau Hombourg invited me to France. He personally took me into the Alsace region to show me the early medieval churches where the tribe of Dan left their footprint. Hence, I saw with my own eyes their pagan and noted symbols within the chapels: The Abbatial Church of Andlau and the Abbey Church of ST Richard.

Unlike other cathedrals in these stand a beautifully large carved wood statue of Sampson wearing a lion skin. In addition to the symbols of the pagan gods of the day, which Dan no doubt worshipped.

Evidence of the Tribe of Dan in Alsace recorded in the Hortus Deliciarum

Further evidencing the tribe of Dan's presence in the heart of Europe is an illustration in the Hortus Deliciarum. Noted as the first illustrated Encyclopedia, it was written between 1159 and 1175. Assembled by a nun named Herrod of Landsberg at Mont Sainte-Odile in Alsace France, it compiled 12 century knowledge. Moreover, she too lists among the relatives of Count Christian d'Andlau Hombourg's family.

One of the labeled illustrations depicts "the taking of the city of Dan." There is no direct verse regarding the attack on Dan by Tiglath Pileser, King of Assyria, in 732 BCE. This had to have been added due to the oral history that was given by the Danites in the family and region.

Count Christian d'Andlau Hombourg identified the Lion of Bashan as a symbol of the Tribe

Count Christian d'Andlau Hombourg pointed out to me the many times the symbol of the lion of Bashan, the tribe used as its symbol. It is thanks to him that I realized the Lion of Bashan is a title for the Antichrist previously omitted among the many Biblical titles. Theologians refer to the Antichrist as simply "the lion" when the lion of Bashan provides the full meaning.

Lion of Bashan a Symbol of the Danites

The Danites adopted the lion of Bashan as one of their symbols. Their footprint left behind in the Alsace region of France is exciting for students of Bible Prophecy. We know the Danites migrated to other parts of Europe based on their names. In Alsace we see actual insights into the Danites and their migration into Europe. It supports what other Scriptures have revealed that the Antichrist will not only rise from the Tribe of Dan but emerge from today's modern Europe. It also negates the writers' who have focused on Dan's migration to Ireland and the UK as the only EU countries the Antichrist can rise from.

About Alsace

Within Alsace are the two churches that bear the marks of the tribe of Dan. One of which also bears symbols of the Templars. In addition, there is Mont Sainte-Odile founded by Adalrich, Duke of Alsace in honor of his daughter, Saint Odile. Along with Andlau Castles, and the burial ground and mausoleum bearing the family's royal crest, for the Andlau family, lies Strasbourg.

Strasbourg was also the seat of the Reformation, and home to John Calvin. It is the largest city in Alsace and located on the border with Germany. Moreover, it is home to the European Parliament building, along with other EU organizations. The building is based on a drawing of the tower of Babel. Constructed as a huge circle, a major demonic stronghold with the force of steel presides over it.

A Final Proof Antichrist will Arise from Europe

When we look at the empires that are associated with Satan and the Antichrist, they are all hubs for international trade. These include Tyre, Babylon and the empire that launches the Antichrist. There is a correlation to trade with Satan and the Antichrist. We see this in the following passages:

- Ezekiel 27:12-23 The King of Tyre- first names the merchants.
- Ezekiel 27: 24 lists the many goods that traded in Tyre and begins with purple clothes.
- Isaiah 14: 12-22 The King of Babylon-

- Revelation 18- Whore of Babylon- details all the goods that traded and concludes the list with, "bodies and souls of men."

Babylon is viewed both in its earlier and later times. In all of my work I have provided the many reasons why the European Union, which is a hub for trade, is the revived Roman empire in which the Antichrist will come to power and lead it to its pinnacle of power.

The Antichrist's childhood and person

It has been written that Satanists are awaiting the son of Satan. One wonders if there have existed any Satanic groups in Europe who might have been aware of his birth. Even they could not imagine what was really coming, which the following pages will detail. As this is not just an ordinary demon but an archangel who commands many other demons. We can only image what his childhood would be like.

The Antichrist will no doubt talk directly to Satan. From childhood he will lead a double life. From an early age he would be interested in politics. He will be cunning, deceitful, smart and an opportunist. He will gain his position through Satan. The book of Revelation state this. He obtains the kingdom through deceit. This is forecast in the book of Daniel. He will also be hungry for power. The Antichrist will appear as an ordinary man. The Bible tells us that he is rude, and he stands out from his peers.

He might not be who you expect

In human terms many expect the Antichrist to be young, charming, and handsome. The Antichrist can in fact be old and unattractive when he takes position. We do not know and are not told. We must remember that Satan is the father of lies. He is a deceiver. He could make the Antichrist old when he gets into power so that no one would suspect.

Yes, the Antichrist could already be in politics for some time now. The Scriptures never describe him as charming, rather that he is arrogant. He becomes strong with a small people. What is certain is that his father is the Devil. He will rise from the tribe of Dan. It might not be obvious he is Jewish. While he looks human, he is not completely. Those with spiritual insight will see a vile spirit within him and in his features.

Jewish Messiah

According to Harper, the early church fathers agreed on another point, and that is that the Antichrist will be Jewish and be accepted by the Jews as the Messiah. Jesus's one direct reference about the Antichrist is that he would be accepted. When Emmanuel Macron became president of France newspapers hailed him as Jupiter. He is the mythological god that most compare to God. We will see the same headlines regarding the Antichrist. Only he will be compared to the Messiah.

The Jews believe that the Messiah can appear suddenly on the scene. In addition, that he will be a great political and military leader, will restore Jerusalem, and rebuild the temple. Finally, that he will usher in peace. All of which is predicted as actions on the part of the Antichrist. Thus, fulfilling Jesus's prediction of the one coming in his own name who will be accepted by the Jews. But what is it that will give the Antichrist this notoriety?

The Peace Treaty

The Antichrist's peace treaty, the one that is

forecast that begins the Tribulation, will mimic the Abrahamic covenant. The Antichrist will both promise Israel peace and safety and guarantee it. The Scripture tells us he signs a seven-year covenant, this most likely will promise military and financial support. The time frame for this aid is seven years according to the Bible, the duration of the Tribulation.

Ezekiel 38-39 War

The Ezekiel 38-39 war, which is a Russian Arab coalition that strikes Israel, will give the Antichrist his opportunity to come to Israel's aid. It would also allow him to take a stand for Israel despite two state solution policy. Most likely the Palestinians will be in on the attack. This will change public opinion against them.

The Antichrist coming to Israel's aid with promise of peace for the nation will help him gain the Jew's favor. Most likely the great earthquake that is predicted that defeats the coalition will destroy the Al-Aqsa mosque. The Antichrist will allow the Third Temple to be rebuilt. Given all of the above When the Jews learn of Antichrist's Jewish ancestry, they will hail him as the Messiah. At this time there will be two types of Jews in Israel, the righteous and unrighteous. They will know the Antichrist's real identity. This of course with the help of the 144 thousand Jewish Evangelists.

The Antichrist Has No Soul

The Antichrist will be a vile person with no regard for anyone. This is because he will lack a soul. Imagine someone without a soul? Instead he is possessed by a major demonic entity: an arch angel. What do you think this means for mankind? All the evilest world leaders and dictators still had souls. Imagine how much worse it could have been if on top of their being evil they lacked a soul. God regards the Antichrist as the 'wicked profane prince.' Archangels are regarded as princes.

We know he is here because of all the signs that are now in place. In addition to the exponential growth in technology, which also indicates he is on this earth.

While writing this book, the COVID plague has swept the globe along with riots, from BLM to many others. In addition, super high record-breaking temperatures in Siberia occurred, and locust plagues in Africa and India. The threat of other illness loom, like

Bubonic. Three hundred and fifty elephants dropped dead, and a swarm of flying ants over the UK showed up on radar. Not to mention devastating floods in Sicily and other extreme weather.

Meanwhile 90K Jews in a short period of time from around the world have applied to go back to Israel. According to an Orthodox Jewish friend of mine in New York City, the consensus is that America has changed after these events, they do not feel the country is the same or in a good direction and are applying to go to Israel. This is no doubt the unfolding of prophecy as God continues to bring the Jews into their own land as He promised. In time for the final seven-year period of their history.

Yet as shocking as all of this on the acceleration of the signs, what the following pages will reveal is the absolute horror and power of the Antichrist and the full meaning of 666, the number of his name.

9 THE SCIENCE OF GOD-ANGELS-DEMONS-666

To get the full impact of the powers of the Antichrist, we are going to look at the Science of God and Demons. Just as Jesus was also God, with all the power of God, but was still a man, the Antichrist possesses all demonic capabilities but is also a man.

In the beginning of this work I shared my experience with both demons and the heavenly realm. This provides the basis for some of the characteristics of demons the following section will reveal. In addition, it will lead to understanding the full meaning of 666, the number of the Antichrist's name and the Mark of the Beast. This is found in Revelation 13:18, which states: "Here is wisdom. Let him who has understanding calculate the number of the beast, for it is the number of a man: His number is 666." Many have written that solving the riddle is simple as counting the letters in a name. This was until technology. The hidden and yet obvious truth is shocking. To understand we must first look to the science of God.

The Science of God

While scientists have erroneously theorized that the earth started with a big bang, the Bible provides the details. Genesis 1:1 states that "the spirit of God was hovering over the surface of the waters." 1 Col 1:17, tells us that He holds all things together. Hebrews 11:3 declares that "the things that are seen are not made of things that are visible." And in this verse and many others we learn that the world was created and framed by the Word of God.

John 1:1 states, "In the beginning was the word and the word was God." The provides another example of simplistic language that is loaded with scientific information.

The Bible makes it clear that God's voice is like thunder. When God speaks think of powerful invisible atomic waves and an incomprehensible force of energy. In addition to possible particles in those waves.

We see in the Bible that around God are forces in nature. In God's throne room, an emerald ring is described encircling His throne. Revelation 4: 2-3 records, "Immediately I was in the Spirit; and behold, a throne set in heaven, and One sat on the throne. And He who sat there was like a jasper and a sardius stone in appearance; and there was a rainbow around the throne, in appearance like an emerald." Jasper and sardius are a burnt orange color like the sun when it begins to set.

Think of these colors like the orange and red that surround Jupiter, which is created by gases. Concerning the emerald rainbow-like ring, the earth has a green glow at night. Just recently, according to Mike Wall, the senior science writer of Space.com in his article, "Weird Green Glow Spotted in Atmosphere of Mars." The European Space Agency's Trace Gas Orbiter, (TGO) spotted an emerald glow in Mar's atmosphere, marking the first time this phenomenon has been spotted beyond the Earth.

It is the green glow of oxygen and is like

Earth's. Multicolored displays are known as auroras, which are generated by charged particles from the sun slamming into the molecules high up in the atmosphere. Day glow arises when the sun's light energy excites atoms and molecules such as nitrogen and oxygen. The glow of God's throne is greater than any of the planets.

The throne room is also depicted as having lightening, for which there is evidence for lightening like discharges on Jupiter, with the electrical currents expected to be ten to 100 times larger than in Earth lightening. The Scripture also refers to thundering coming from the throne, this occurs from the shockwaves, according to the Plasma Coalition in their report, *About Plasma's:*

"The electrical current in a lightning flash varies from stroke to stroke as well as during each stroke. The return-stroke current rises rapidly to an initial peak of tens of thousands of amperes. That initial current pulse may be followed by a current of hundreds of amperes lasting for tens of thousandths of a second. The high return-stroke current rapidly heats the channel to a peak temperature near or above 50,000°F, increasing the pressure in the channel to ten or more times normal atmospheric pressure. This makes the channel produce the intense light that we see and makes it expand, producing a shock wave that eventually becomes the thunder sound wave we hear in the distance."

Around God's throne is heavenly thunder and lightning of incredible power. Science has discovered electrical currents throughout outer space of immense strength. These findings are recorded in the book *Electric Currents in Geospace and Beyond* published in 2018.

On the creation, it should be noted that Genesis written in 950 BC tells us that in heaven is a large body of water that existed before the formation of the earth. Psalm 148: 2-6 references the water in the heavens. Many regarded this as Biblical fables.

In July of 2011, NASA reported that astronomers found the largest, most distant reservoir of water ever detected in the universe. They estimate that the water is equivalent to 140 trillion times all the water in the world's ocean. It surrounds a huge feeding black hole called a quasar.

Creation of the Angels

Just as God's throne has an atomic composition, so also do demons and angels. In the Bible angels and demons are referred to as stars. Stars also emit electricity and light. Angels were created and exist in the unseen or atomic realm. According to Job 38:4-7, God created the angels first and they applauded his creation of the earth and man. In Psalm 148: 2-6 it states they were spoken into existence. When you think of God's voice, it equates to a powerful subatomic wave. Demons are a combination of particles and waves.

Creation of Man-More Personal

This differs from the creation of man who God formed him out of the dust of the earth and breathed into him the breath of life. A woman he formed from the rib of Adam.

From the passage we see that angels are lumped in with the heavens. Their composition would give them extraordinary capabilities, in which they would act as God's servants. The creation of man involved God fashioning him with His hands and breathing into his mouth, which is more personal than the creation of the angels reflecting the relational aspect of God and man. The angel's capabilities would leave Satan, the highest one with the idea that he himself could surpass God. One can only imagine the knowledge that Satan was given by God, enough so that he felt that he could rise above God.

Demons Like the Stars

Demons are called stars and equated to them. There is the possibility that from the creation of each star in the force of energy of the nuclear fusion birthed a spirit or angel and the power of the angel would depend on the star and its size. Angels are known to emit light like a star.

A Fact About Stars

In November of 2018, the Jet Propulsion Laboratory of the California Institute of Technology wrote that NASA's Spitzer Space Telescope reported that for the first-time silica, one of the most common minerals found on earth is formed when massive stars explode. It is found in 60% of the earth's crust and is throughout the universe.

Transparent Element

Silica or silicon dioxide makes up 95% of rocks, is a form of quartz and is also found in tissues in the human body. It is also found in plants and drinking water. Silica is also used to make glass. It is interesting that glass which is made from silica and quartz have a transparent element, like angels and demons. There is some relation there.

Demons and Electricity

In Luke 10:18 it quotes Jesus as saying, "I saw Satan fall like lightning from heaven. Stars produce lightening. Lightening is also equated to electricity. There is a relation of the demonic realm to electricity. We also see that in the throne room of God is electricity and all throughout outer space are electrical currents. Peter Dockrill reported in February 2020 that "Scientists Built A Genius Device That Generates Electricity Out of Thin Air. They produced it from a bacteria.

Another device written about in the American Institute of Physics was able to generate electricity from the coldness of the universe. Demons are attracted to water and electricity can flow through water. Because water caries impurities these can enable a small number of ions to conduct electrical current.

Electricity in the Human Body

In addition, demons inhabit human bodies and our bodies carry electricity. Human cells conduct electrical current. At rest a human produces 100 watts of power, and with very short bursts of energy such as sprinting can output over 2,000 watts.

Amber Plante University of Maryland Graduate School stated, "Electricity is everywhere, even in the human body. Our cells are specialized to conduct electrical currents. Electricity is required for the nervous system to send signals throughout the body and to the brain, making it possible for us to move, think and feel."

Life is in the Blood

The Bible says the life is in the blood. Blood also has an electrical component. In addition, scientists in Russia are working on creating small batteries for pacemakers powered by the energy from a person's own blood. This is based on the same idea of waterfalls that generate power. Blood also carries oxygen to all parts of the body and thus its relation to air.

Somehow within our blood is a subatomic layer of waves and particles that make our soul or spirit. Both angels and the spirit man once created never die. Only our physical body's will experience death. We see at the judgment both are not destroyed but rather cast into the lake of fire for eternity. Meanwhile the souls of men destined for the Lake of Fire await the Judgment in Hades. In addition, various demons are chained in the abyss.

Somehow the life is related to the energy that is also capable of conducting electricity in our bodies. In the blood electrolytes are an example.

The Brain and Neurons

The brain also fires neurons, or electrical charges. There are already algorithms that can get an idea of your thoughts based on the electrical impulses.

A human thought results as the brain neurons fire and relay electrical signals called 'action potential'. Ions flow in and out of the neuron. These are electrical impulses and temporary shifts from positive to negative. Demons can read and understand these impulses, which is how they can read your thoughts. In addition to put thoughts into your head. They can possibly do this by manipulating the brain firing to put in the thought. This can ultimately guide one's actions.

There is no parallel universe

Scientists theorize there is a parallel universe or even multiverses that exist alongside of our universe. Some believe that demons and angels existed in this realm. The truth is there is no parallel universe. Demons and angels exist within our universe right beside of us. If this were not the case, the Nephilim would not have been able to cohabitate with the daughters of men.

Limited Eyesight

The reason that we do not see demons is because our eyesight is limited in how we see objects and which ones we see. In 2007 MIT discovered that to make an item invisible you bend light around it. This was published in

MIT Technology Review, *How to Make an Object Invisible* by Dunkan Graham-Rowe. Demons reflect light around them so that they cannot be seen with the naked eye. Or the light goes through them in another way that cannot be seen by our vision. This means that our eyesight is limited. The human eye can only see items in which light reflects in specific directions.

The Demonic Eyes

Although demon spirits have a level of transparency they have faces and bodies. When a demon inhabits someone, they can show through the eyes and partially through the features because as they inhabit the person's body their light deflection gets altered. So, you will see the demonic eyes very clearly though the person's eyes. In addition to seeing some semblance of the person's facial features merged with the demons.

The Third Eye

New Age and occult teachings teach about the third eye, which is the pineal gland. Ancient Egypt taught about the eye of Horus or Ra and giving someone a good eye or an evil eye. It was also thought to provide magic to living users. The idea is that the third eye is the doorway to all things psychic.

The truth is that in the garden man had another set of eyes that could see all beings, but Satan got Eve to eat from the tree of the knowledge of good and evil, which was a DNA changing tree. This changed man's eyesight. We see from the Bible that the change was not instant it took about 800 to 1000 years for the final deteriorated state. Therefore, the early patriarchs were able to see into the spiritual realm.

When the final deterioration of man's body was complete God had to give eyes to see heavenly beings. This is recorded in 2 Kings 6:17: "And Elisha prayed, and said, "LORD, I pray, open his eyes that he may see." Then the LORD opened the eyes of the young man, and he saw. And behold, the mountain was full of horses and chariots of fire all around Elisha.

The Original Earth and the Garden

In the Garden of Eden, Adam and Eve were created to have direct fellowship with God. There was no sickness or death. In addition, man's eyesight allowed him to see the entire world that lay before him. The earth was also different. It did not rain in the earth before the flood. Dinosaurs were able to exist.

When the fall took place, it changed man so that he would now sin, and physically die. But it took time for the change to wear down the originally designed body. Early man lived over 800 years. His eyesight still allowed him to see the spiritual world, this too eroded with time. Man would be separated from God and accept Him through faith alone.

The Nephilim in Early Period of the Fall

It was in this time frame that Enoch walked with God and that the fallen angels had sexual intercourse with the daughters of men. These women gave birth to giants. The Hebrew word in the Bible "nephiyl" is uncertain and means fallers, rebels, apostates. Other definitions of the word are a bully a tyrant, feller, fierce, cruel, dreadful, savage from naphal, to fall.

The word also relates to the giant star constellation Orion. Fallen like fallen stars, and the angels are referred to as stars. These fallen angels were still easily able to be seen by the women they cohabitated with. This is because the vision into the spiritual realm had not completely deteriorated. The fallen angels appeared like men.

In that Demons can cause illness, they were able to supercharge some aspects of the DNA so that the offspring would grow into giants. A woman's body was in a different state than today lending to this ability. The offspring were part demonic, and God had the Israelite's destroy each one of them.

Demons are Cold

It is generally accepted that demons are cold. As I relayed at the beginning of this work, it is what I had experienced. According to PC Magazine's "7 Surprising Ghost Hunting Gadgets" and what they refer to as ghosts are demons:

"A simple thermometer, when used for ghost hunting becomes a cold-spot detector to identify small pockets of cooler air, which to ghost hunters indicate the presence of a ghost. For more sizable shifts, some use earthquake-detecting seismographs to alert them to the presence of the paranormal."

"For the most part the equipment we use is to monitor the environment," Griffith says. Ghost hunters use anything that can track and monitor temperature, electromagnetic fields, static charge changes, barometric pressure and wind changes. "It is not normal for any of these environmental conditions to change drastically in a short period of time." He says. "We have found that when this happens paranormal activity is underway."

Demons are in the Air

Paul refers to Satan as the Prince of the power of the air. Ephesians 2:1-2 tells us, "And you were dead in your trespasses and sins, in which you formerly walked according to the course of this world, according to the prince of the power of the air, of the spirit that is now working in the sons of disobedience."

The prince of the power of the air refers to demons and demon spirits that cannot be seen but are in the air. As I stated we cannot see them because our vision is limited. They exist in the atomic scale, meaning they are made of subatomic particles. They are either a wave or a particle.

Demons and the Quantum Realm

Demons can occupy two states at the same time. While both unseen, they can also be seen by in their realm. They can exist in multiple places at the same time and can also take physical form. Their molecular state can shift and recreate itself to an extent. While I have just described the science behind the Demon, it is also the science behind Quantum Computing and particle physics.

Cold of Demons & Quantum Computing

Demons like water, and bodies to inhabit. But they can also be around objects, and they are also extremely cold. Quantum Computing is operating at extremely low temperatures.
 According to Entering the strange world of ultra-cold chemistry by the Georgia Institute of Technology dated, November 2, 2015, "The reason is because absolute zero is the temperature at which all thermal activity stops. At the exceptionally low temperatures, atoms and molecules move much more slowly and have different kind of interactions." In addition, at the cold temperatures there is no wave interference, and the wavelengths become larger as the temperature drops.

Ultra-Cold Chemistry

In conventional chemistry, activation barriers must be overcome before atoms can exchange electrons to bind together. Because they have so little energy at ultra-cold temperatures, atoms cannot overcome this activation barrier, meaning interactions must occur through other mechanisms - including quantum tunneling effects. Superconducting must be conducted at a super cold state.

Quantum Tunneling

Another aspect of quantum mechanics that mirrors what we know about demons is quantum tunneling. This occurs when particles move through a barrier that, according to the theories of classical physics should be impossible to move through. This is in part because particles can behave like waves. It also describes the actions of spirits.

Particles-Waves-Superposition

Quantum physics did the double slit test experiment using light to see if it was both a wave and a particle. They discovered the wave particle duality and that every particle is also a wave. They also discovered that these waves and particles can occupy two places at once. They call this quantum superposition.

The same two atoms can also exist in two places nearly two feet apart simultaneously. As Scientists made findings in the quantum realm, they discovered what they did not expect which is the great capabilities of those particles. Quantum particles go into two states at once and can be hot and cold at the same time. Scientists are not sure where these two states go. They go into the angelic and demonic realm.

This is also portrayed in the Bible as the nature of God, only he is everywhere at once. Only God exists on a smaller subatomic scale. Meanwhile quantum takes us into the demonic realm. From these discovery's scientists can literally recreate what are considered miracles.

Quantum Discovers Demonic Realm Demons are in the gods

The word for demons in the Greek is Daimon and it means god or goddess. An inferior deity, whether good or bad in the NT, an evil spirit.

A supernatural spirit of a bad nature. The Scripture is clear that the demons re in the idols. Technology is one of society's gods Quantum Computing is entering the demonic realm and merging the demonic world with the physical.

Revelation's Quantum Language

Revelation 17 in two verses repeats quantum mechanics language. Revelation 17:8 states:

"The beast you saw was, and is not, and will ascend out of the bottomless pit and go to perdition. And those who dwell on the earth will marvel, whose names are not written in the Book of Life from the foundation of the world, when they see the beast that was, and is not , and yet is."

Quantum Discovers Demonic Realm Demons are in the gods

The word for demons in the Greek is Daimon and it means god or goddess. An inferior deity, whether good or bad in the NT, an evil spirit. A supernatural spirit of a bad nature. The Scripture is clear that the demons re in the idols. Technology is one of society's gods

Quantum Computing is entering the demonic realm. In the Scripture we also see this duality again with the mark of the beast. It is both hidden and obvious at the same time.

The God Particle-Higgs Boson

When the Scientists at CERN discovered the Higgs Boson particle the media hailed it as the God particle. Scientists stated this was exaggerated and inaccurate They hoped to discover the particle that created the Big Bang, which is an erroneous theory and they will never find it.

Smaller Particles Than Higgs Boson

What scientists will find is smaller particles and even smaller ones that their microscopes are not capable of seeing or providing the magnification. The Times of India reported in 2014 that Scientists announced the possibility of a particle smaller than the Higgs Boson. They referenced "particles" meaning more than one.

According to the article, "The entire Standard Model also rests on the existence of a special kind of particle: the Higgs particle. This particle originates from an invisible field that fills up all space. Even when the universe seems empty this field is there. Without it, we would not exist, because it is from the contact with the field that particles acquire mass." This mirrors the Biblical verse how the universe is held together. Moreover, with each of the particles that get smaller such as quarks, scientists find smaller particles yet.

Benoit Mandelbrot-fractal discoveries

Mathematician Benoit Mandelbrot presented the fractal geometry of nature. Fractals are a form of geometric repetition in which smaller and smaller copies of a pattern are nested inside each other, so the same intricate shape appears no matter how you zoom in to the whole. From ferns, broccoli, shapes of mountains, river basins, structures of plants, blood vessels, trees, lungs, galaxies and more. There is even this branching out of the Revelation judgements with the trumpets into bowls, into the three woes.

God's Makeup-Fractal

It is a possibility that the makeup of God is

fractal in nature. That he is made of atomic particles and waves that continue into even smaller particles, that do not end. It is from these particles and waves that branch like a tree and go smaller and smaller that represent a God that has no beginning, or end, who does not fill space and yet fills it. A God who from these unseen particles and waves can create whatever He chooses and be everywhere at once, while also appearing as a burning bush, or as a still small voice.

This describes what the book of Hebrews states that from the unseen comes that which we can see. The atomic particles that make up God are infinitely smaller and smaller and go for infinity. It is why Jesus stated in John 8:48-49, "Before Abraham was I am." God is all space, with no beginning or end.

Scientist Yaniv Stern's Discovery

Biological Scientist Yaniv Stern PHD from the University of Leeds, is challenging some of the scientific standard teachings regarding weight and mass. He stated on his website: "The theory of evolution has reduced all of biological diversity to a single cell, a mere lipid vesicle encapsulating a short random RNA.

When I broke this cell further down through its constituent molecules and atoms at the sub atomic level I discovered increasing complexity with many elementary particles and forces and this did not make sense to me."

In addition, Stern concluded: "I felt that as matter is broken down, further and further, fewer elementary particles and forces should exist, the simpler the rules of science should become."

God Holds All Things Together

Most likely the field Scientists talk about that holds everything together is God. The Bible even affirms the fact that God hold all things together.

The God symbol is a tree, which is a fractal, and is flowing and continuous, and represents life. Satan's main symbol is a circle, which is closed, confines, and does not flow but signifies death.

God Vs Angels Demons

The quantum realm that scientists have discovered is the world of demons and their abilities, where the impossible can be viewed and duplicated. The God infinity, fractal particles help to put the angelic and demonic in perspective to God's power.

God Speaks-Waves

When God spoke the angels into existence, he released waves. Demons are particles and waves, or both or one or the other. This is in line with what we know about their creation. In Ephesians 2:2 Paul states that Satan is the prince of the power of the air. This means that he uses these demons to accomplish his purposes. Satan uses more than the demons of the air. When you think of radio and cell phone towers that work on air waves, according to this verse, this is Satan's domain. This is also the power of the air.

6G Air Waves

6 G works on what is called Sub 6, 600 MHz to 6 GHz also used by 4G LTE but will also use a higher band of GHz from 24 to 86, much higher frequencies bring much higher data rates. While it can carry higher data, it can't carry it as far, so it uses small cells and many more towers. These small cells also use

beamforming. It also uses electromagnetic fields and radio waves. 6 G will move away from wires and the. Internet and cell phone network become the same thing.

6 Genesis-Nephilim

In Finland, a company is working on the 6Genesis Flagship program. It is a recently formed Finnish academic and industrial consortium aiming at developing key enabling technologies for 6G. 6GFP is an eight-year large-scale research initiative set to ultimately develop, implement, and test key enabling technologies for 6G.

Of all names 6 Genesis? In Genesis chapter 6 is the reference to the Nephilim.

6G and Quantum

Quantum Computing will be able to help data bases access all kinds of information at lightning speed, and 6 G will deliver it instantaneously without any wires. Concerning 6G and quantum, Andy Boxall stated in his article, *What is 6G It could make 5G look like 2G, but its not even close to reality*. He stated,

"Forget one movie downloading in a few seconds from Netflix with 5G, with 6G speeds like that, in just one second you could download 142 hours of Netflix movies. It may also bring about sci-fi applications like the integration of our brains with computers, and greatly improved touch control systems. NTT DoCoMo talks about 6G making it, "possible for cyberspace to support human thought and action in real time through wearable devices and micro-devices mounted on the human body."

Demonic Influence Arts and Science

In the beginning of this book I told how I saw a demon over someone who later began drawing variations of the demon. There was the young man who drew a tattoo design that was the demon that was over him that came through on his face. As I stated demons can read our thoughts and influence them via the firing of the neurons and the electrical impulses. No doubt demons will both influence and continues to aid the minds of the scientists as they develop 6G and Quantum Computing.

Verse in Daniel Predicts Quantum

Daniel 11:38-39 references the Antichrist and technology and states, "But in his estate shall he honor the God of forces: and a god whom his fathers knew not shall he honor with gold, and silver, and with precious stones, and pleasant things. Thus, shall he do in the most strong holds with a strange god whom he shall acknowledge and increase with glory: and he shall cause them to rule over many and shall divide the land for gain."

According to this verse the Antichrist is honoring demons. Based on this verse this is a stronghold with a chief demon and the plural of "cause them to rule over many." This is a stronghold. The Antichrist is the archangel over this, a chief demon is underneath him. Below the demon are many spirits. All of these that power the quantum computer.

Technology Fortress

The term God of forces means fortress and the word used for God, is the same as for the God of the Bible. This is because it will have God like qualities. In addition, technology will act as a fortress by giving information on any who might oppose the empire.

The Image of the Beast

Quantum Computing goes into the demonic realm as does 6 G. It creates an environment for demons to operate. Even more so the most frightening aspect of quantum computing and 6G is that it will provide a replica of the Antichrist in the physical realm. It is truly the image of the Beast.

If we examine Revelation 13:18 considering this knowledge, the meaning is now clear. In addition, as I stated, it is both hidden and obvious at the same time. It reads, "Here is wisdom. Let him who has understanding calculate the number of the beast, for it the number of a man: His number is 666."

The most frightening aspect quantum computing and 6G is that it will provide a replica of the Antichrist in the physical realm. It is truly the image of the Beast.

This is 666

666 is the combination of 6G at 600 MHz, with most likely a 66-cubit computer. The largest quantum computer right now is 53 cubits.

6G utilizes the power of the air, which is controlled by Satan. The combination of both quantum and 6G would give Antichrist God like power in the physical realm. But even more frightening is it is him, a replica of him. Computing will not just be man merging with machines, but quantum is the marriage of demons with machines or replicating themselves in demon form. The computer will then be merged with man.

The Meaning of 666 the number of his name

In my book decoding 666, I wrote about how being numbered in the Bible equates death, in addition how by taking the mark of the beast you will blaspheme the Holy Spirit. Here we add the final piece that by taking the Mark of the Beast, you are taking the Antichrist in the same way one would accept Christ. Finally, 666, this all-knowing machine in the physical realm blasphemes the trinity and is a replica of him.

News For Quantum Sceptics

There are quantum sceptics who write that

Quantum computing will never be realized. That it is not possible. Several companies already unveiled a quantum computer, with Honeywell being the latest.

There already exists the Quantum Internet Alliance, which is already at work to provide the network for quantum computers to connect them. In addition to quantum software designers there are also code writers who are working on the code for the quantum internet.

In June 2019 seven EU members agreed to work together to make available a quantum communication infrastructure. At a digital assembly they signed a declaration: Belgium, Germany, Italy, Luxembourg, Malta, the Netherlands, and Spain. The Quantum internet alliance is funded by the European Union's Quantum Technologies Flagship.

Worldwide mandate for the mark of the beast

A key Revelation prophecy is that the Antichrist will set up an image of himself and institute the mark of the beast.

The Antichrist is most known for the mark of the beast. The Antichrist will use technology to monitor all people, but also to put his thoughts into you. To lead and guide his followers. Technology will give the Antichrist God like powers in the physical realm. Through technology he will be like God on this earth.

666 Number of Antichrist and Unholy Trinity

The Bible tells us in Revelation 13:18 that 666 is the number of a man. The technology sums him up and his aims, it is his equation in the physical realm. It is the number of the unholy trinity and of idolatry. The technology is the full manifestation of Satan in the physical realm.

Daniel 3: 1-25 Nebuchadnezzar's Golden Image

Nebuchadnezzar's golden image is a replica of the Antichrists. The prophet Daniel told Nebuchadnezzar concerning his dream image that he was the head of gold (Daniel 2:38). Thus the gold is a replica of Nebuchadnezzar. In addition, there were six instruments played when people were to worship the image. Music equates to math just like physics, where the science is mathematical. In addition, music produces waves.

This is identical to the mark of the beast technology, and like Nebuchadnezzar's golden image of 60 cubits, and 6 cubits, and six instruments. So too will the Antichrist's image have 600 from one technology and 66 from another combined. Nebuchadnezzar's image provides verification this speculation of the image of the Beast is correct.

Tyre, Babylon Places of Trade-Technology

In the Bible Satan is associated with Tyre and Babylon and Trade. Both passages are quite detailed as I stated in an earlier chapter. The EU is also known for trade, which is where the Antichrist will rise from and lead the EU empire.

The AI White Paper-Quantum Flagship

The European Union is determined to win the race in the next leap in technology. This is to ensure economic prosperity of the Union. Wealth equals power. For this the EU issued in Feb 2020 the White Paper on AI.

In addition, as of October 2018, the European Commission is funding the Quantum Flagship. This is the third largest research and innovation initiative after the Graphene Flagship and the Human Brain Project. This is all part of the Horizon 2020 program, which invested 80 billion euros over a seven-year period ending this year in 2020.

The Antichrist Will Have Direct Line to Technologies.

All these technologies have a direct line to the Commission president of the EU. There is even a commissioner under the president over technology. This means that the Antichrist will have direct knowledge of the latest technologies.

King of Tyre-Mystery Verse Meaning

There is an ambiguous passage in Ezekiel 28 talking about Satan as the King of Tyre. It reads in Ezekiel 28:16, "By the abundance of your trading you became filled with violence within."

The word for violence also includes

oppression. Revelation 13:17 states, "And that no man might buy or sell, save he that had the mark, or the name of the beast, or the number of his name."

Buying and selling is trading. The mark of the beast is oppression or violence through trade. It becomes the requirement to buy and sell. With the EU's Quantum Flagship and the White Paper on AI, it has determined that it will take the lead in the next technological leap. This means prosperity for the EU Empire, and it ensures its prosperity through trade. In addition, it prepares for the Antichrist unbeknownst to the citizens and politicians. We know from Bible Prophecy that the European Union will in fact win the technological race. They will launch both Quantum and 6 G. Only, this is not an ordinary technology, it replicates the Antichrist and his demonic dominion. Most likely these will be launched after the Tribulation begins and not beforehand.

10 WHAT THIS MEANS FOR THE TRIBULATION SAINTS

You can only imagine the horror of the believers living during the Tribulation. They will know that the Antichrist is the son of Satan. They will also understand that this technology, this thing is an electronic replica of him with all his demons below him in charge of the technology.

Blasphemy of the Trinity Via the Mark

By taking the mark, they take him into their bodies but more so into their hearts and lives. He will merge with them and be able to put his thoughts into them. His image will know every move, every purchase, every search on the internet and all about them. It will give him God like powers. More so through it he will blaspheme the Trinity via this technology. The technology's capability to be all knowing mimics God the father. The fact that one must accept the technology in the way they accept Jesus by a decision of their and view the Antichrist as a sort of savior mimics Jesus Christ.

As one accepts Christ and believes on Him, so also will they do with the Antichrist. As the Holy Spirit seals and guides one, so also will the mark. The Antichrist might be able to put thoughts into you and guide you.

Blasphemy of the Holy Spirit

But the Antichrist will blaspheme the Holy Spirit.

Understanding the Unforgiveness of the Blasphemy of the Holy Spirit

One must question why the blasphemy of the Holy Spirit is such a bad sin that there is no forgiveness. Theologians all primarily agree that it is the rejection of the Lord Jesus Christ that is the unforgivable sin. But rejecting the Gospel or Jesus is not blasphemy. Many have reverence and respect for God and Jesus without giving their hearts. To understand we need to look to the Old Testament.

We see that anyone who looked on God's face would die.

Exodus 33:20 records, "But He said, "you cannot see my face; for no man shall see Me and live."

What becomes a pattern is that there are aspects to God that are so powerful its beyond our comprehension. Such as looking at God's face and dying. We see similar with touching the Ark of the Covenant. The Bible records the story of Uzzah. who touched the Ark of the Covenant and died because God killed him. A detail that adds to the severity of the touch is that the man accidentally touched it (2 Samuel 6:1-7, 1 Chronicles 13:9-12).

Then there is the story of the Philistines capturing the Ark that 1 Samuel 4-7 records. The Philistines brought the Ark and placed it in front of their god Dagon. He was the half man half fish fertility god of the Philistines. The next day the god lay prostrate, had fallen in front of the ark as if worshiping it. They put him upright again and found him the following morning on the ground again in front of the ark, this time with his head and hands broken off. With Demons in the idols, no doubt, this is a powerful illustration of God's authority. It also reminds me of Jesus when he stated in Luke 19:40, "But He answered them and said to them, 'I tell you that if these should keep silent, the stones would immediately cry out."

As the Philistines moved the ark God afflicted them with tumors and soon, they got the message and returned the Ark with a sin offering of golden tumors and mice.

We see also those who take the Antichrist's mark, God plagues with ugly and painful sores (Revelation 16:1).

So from these passages we see aspects of God's holiness that are off limits to man. When we look at the Holy Spirit we think of the incomprehensible seven spirits of God and the spirits in the wheels of the four living creates. A very Holy aspect of the Holy Spirit is that it was instrumental in the birth of Christ. In addition, our own spiritual rebirth. John 3:6 states, That which is born of flesh is flesh, and that which is born of Spirit is spirt. Truly, truly

I tell you, no one can enter the kingdom of God unless he is born of water and the Spirit. Thus the Spirit seals us, teaches and more. But, the Spirit is this aspect of God and Jesus' holiness that we cannot comprehend. Like the ark or looking into God's face, there is a serious consequence if it is blasphemed.

According to the Bible Blasphemy means, railings reviling's, slander, injurious speech to another's good name. It is probably from blapbo meaning to injure, Speed defamatory of divine majesty, evil speaking, railing.

Revelation 13:6, "And he opened his mouth in blasphemy against God, to blaspheme his name, and his tabernacle and them that dwell in heaven.

Daniel 11: 36 [36] "Then the king shall do according to his own will: he shall exalt and magnify himself above every god, shall speak blasphemies against the God of gods, and shall prosper till the wrath has been accomplished; for what has been determined shall be done. [37] He shall regard neither the [g]God of his fathers nor the desire of women, nor regard any god; for he shall exalt himself above *them* all.

Jesus was accused of blasphemy for saying He was the son of God, by those who did not believe Him. In Revelation 2:9, He referred the blasphemy of those who "say they are Jews, and are not, but are of the synagogue of Satan." We see that the Antichrist's blasphemy does both, it rails against the true God and each member of the Trinity and also claims to be God.

The blasphemy of the Holy Spirit will be not only speaking against but also claiming to provide a new birth through the mark. Sealing those who are his through it. Joining the souls to him. He might even claim to be it as well. He might even be able to put his thought into the person as well as try to guide them. He will tout the all knowingness of the technology as godlike and spirit like.

With this blasphemy of the spirit, anyone who takes the mark becomes unredeemable. If any of them had known Christ and received the spirit it will retreat out of such a person. Revelation 3:5 seems to contradict what the Bible states about salvation, but it is in line with the blasphemy of the spirit. IT states," He who overcomes shall be clothed in white garments, and I will not blot his name from the Book of Life; but I will confess his name before My Father and before His angels.

We cannot imagine what the Antichrist will say that fulfill the blasphemy the Scripture predicts. Just as the Philistines were inflicted with a plague of tumors, those who take the mark and partake in the sin against the Spirit will break out with painful and loathsome sores.

The Mark and its touted benefits

The mark will also prosper the Antichrist's empire economically as it is employed worldwide. In addition, with the crime and immorality at its height, he will come with this technology as the answer to preventing many of the crimes and scams that plague society.

A King of Fierce Countenance

No one can fully imagine the horror of having the world's leading empire ruled by the Son of Satan. Antichrist will lead the European Union. He will appear human, just as Jesus when he walked the earth.

According to Daniel 8:23, he will be a king with a fierce countenance, and will understand dark sentences. Fierce is taken from the Hebrew word As and it means strong, vehement, harsh: fierce, greedy, mighty, power, roughly strong, also impudent, shameless. He will have gained his position through cunning and deceit. This is not surprising as Satan is the father of lies. Demons are lying spirits and the Antichrist is after all a demonic entity. Once he gets into power in the European Union, he will lead it to its height of power. He will make his name as the guardian of Israel. Meanwhile the Revelation plagues will have begun.

Once Antichrist Gets in Power

Daniel 11:23 states that after the league made with him, he acts deceptively. Meaning that after he gets into his position, he makes like he is for the good of the empire but is really building it for the day he stands in the Jewish temple and declares himself as God. Up until this time he will began to change times and laws. He will also be at work on the mark of the beast project, preparing it for launch. He will strong arm nations into adopting EU law and policy.

All 3 Members of Unholy Trinity on Earth

Once the abomination of desolation occurs, and when the Antichrist is killed and rises back to life, afterwards, he will have no restraints. The war in heaven will have taken place between Michael and Satan. Lucifer will be kicked out of the heavens and will be on the earth. All three members of the unholy trinity will be on earth at the same time.

I do not think we can imagine what it will be like having all three of the Satanic entity's on earth simultaneously. The Revelation plagues will occur concurrently. The Bible states after the war in heaven in Revelation 12:12: "Therefore rejoice, ye heavens, and ye that dwell in them. Woe to the inhabitants of the earth and of the sea! for the devil is come down unto you, having great wrath, because he knows that he hath but a short time.?

A woe in the Bible means great judgement. In addition to all of this, the horror of men, women, and children controlled by the mark of the beast. Accepting it as one would Christ.

Believers at the time will know the mark of the

beast is a replica of the Antichrist. They will not only be merged with a machine, but to the demonic hoards under the Antichrist. This means accepting part of his spirit or those he controls into them. He might even call it their new birth. In this he will also blaspheme the spirit.

From Revelation 13 we see that even in the physical realm, the great mark of the beast technological achievement, which also takes them into the demonic realm is limited. God allows the illusion of it being greater in capability. Such as by granting the false prophet power to breath life into the image so that it speaks.

They will also hear his blasphemies and know that by taking the mark, not only are they accepting him as they would accept Christ. but also will blaspheme the Holy Spirit. We cannot even imagine their horror at this, but also their suffering for not taking the mark that will lead to their deaths. We can understand it now, as 666 is the technology and the technology is the Antichrist.

At the time the Antichrist goes into the Third Temple and declares himself as god, no one will be able to defeat him. He will have risen the EU to the height of its power. Between his rising from the dead, or appearing to, and the miracles produced by the false prophet including making the Antichrist's image into a speaking being, many will be deceived into believing his is something great. Whatever their view, the Scripture states that he causes all to take the mark of the beast, which essentially means, "make one do something."

The plague of sores come upon those who do take it for their sin of blasphemy of the Holy Spirit in taking the mark.

Antichrist will change times and laws

In addition, the Bible tells us that the Antichrist will change times and laws. He is described as the lawless one in 2 Thessalonians 2:2. We can only conceptualize the list:

- Legalize pedophilia-incest-child porn
- Allowing all who are deemed criminals to have their organs harvested
- Legalizing the illegal drug trade
- Open the door to all scientific and medical experiments no matter how

unethical including gene editing and human cloning
- Legalize prostitution worldwide
- Eliminate age restrictions on tobacco and alcohol
- Eliminate freedom of speech
- No limits on torture or police brutality
- Beheading of Christians-Jews on alter at the Jewish Temple. Harvesting of organs afterwards.
- Brutal torture of Christian's-Jews to get them to take the mark of the Beast, lasting 10 days.
- Censoring the internet, removing any references to God, Jesus, or any religion other than him.
- Paying those who betray those who do not take the mark of the beast
- Abolishing all religion
- Taking State Possession of all religious buildings and art and selling them
- Public torture
- Public executions
- War for the sake of war
- Evil the mind cannot even imagine being allowed

It can go even further than this, what if he legalized all crime and penalized all acts of goodness.

When we think of dictators in modern history, Hitler, Pol Pot, Stalin, the Antichrist will not compare. As stated, earlier Antichrist has no soul. Put all previous dictators together and the Antichrist rises far above them in power and viciousness. Evil will be ruling the most powerful empire to ever exist. Pure wickedness.

The Prophet Daniel Fainted

The prophet Daniel fainted as the vision of the Antichrist. He described the Antichrist's empire as exceedingly dreadful and frightening. Daniel also could not eat for weeks he was so sick at the revelation.

Mystery of the Early Church Fathers Solved

I understand now, why the early church fathers focused on the Antichrist. In addition, why Jesus taught his disciples about him. Here we are with the fig tree ripening and he is now here on earth.

The realization of the Antichrist as the son of Satan, and what the world is in for under this rule, should make everyone run to Jesus Christ and makes sure they know Him. The Antichrist is already here waiting to take his lead role in the European Union. We will most likely be here once he gets appointed to his political seat. We will also most likely be on earth when he begins to lead. But we will be raptured anytime thereafter once he gets into power. He is in deceiver mode at that time. We cannot imagine the horror he will put the believers though who live under his rule.

The Antichrist is Appointed By God

The Bible emphasizes that the Antichrist arrives when the transgressors are come to the full. While Satan has a plan for his son on earth, God appoints him for his purpose of judging the inhabitants on the earth and bringing an end to this current age. The Antichrist's reign ushers in the battle of Armageddon.

Jeremiah 51 states:

"You *are* My battle-ax *and* weapons of war:

For with you I will break the nation in pieces;
With you I will destroy kingdoms;
With you I will break in pieces the horse and its rider;
With you I will break in pieces the chariot and its rider;
With you also I will break in pieces man and woman;
With you I will break in pieces old and young;
With you I will break in pieces the young man and the maiden;
With you also I will break in pieces the shepherd and his flock;
With you I will break in pieces the farmer and his yoke of oxen;
And with you I will break in pieces governors and rulers.

Arthur Pink's Last Words

Theologian Arthur Pink's last words were, "the Scriptures explain themselves." He was so right, they certainly do. I want to add that from them I have learned that "in their simplicity, is complexity. A few words give light into a vast complex world. The book of John tells us that in the beginning was the Word, and the Word was with God and the Word was God. As the song says, "there is power in the Word." In it are the keys to the universe.

What a privilege for me to take up the torch on the teachings of the Antichrist and examining his arrival, and to be the generation in which he arrives and to know that Jesus's coming is now not far away.

The Hope for Believer's Today

If you know Jesus as your personal savior, the Bible says to believe on the Lord Jesus Christ and thou shalt be saved. Its as simple as believing in Him. Those of us who do have the hope of the Rapture. At this event we will be taken out of the earth just before the Tribulation begins.

A Word to the Tribulation Saints

If you are reading this after the Tribulation has begun, my hope and prayer is that this book will give you the information you need. That it will confirm what you already understand. Just know that after you are brutally murdered, you will be spared the worst of the Revelation judgments and your deaths will be avenged. May Jesus give you strength to endure now what you must endure.

ABOUT THE AUTHOR

Erika Grey, author, Bible scholar, commentator, journalist has been a born-again Christian for over 40 years She has written numerous books on Bible Prophecy and made contributions in helping to decode the more difficult forecasts. She has spoken on numerous radio stations including Coast to Coast.

This book is one of a series of short books by Erika Grey intended to be quick reads with important information. Be sure to check out Erika's other titles at www.erikagrey.com.

www.ingramcontent.com/pod-product-compliance
Lightning Source LLC
Chambersburg PA
CBHW030655230426
43665CB00011B/1103